BE YOUR OWN BACKING BAND

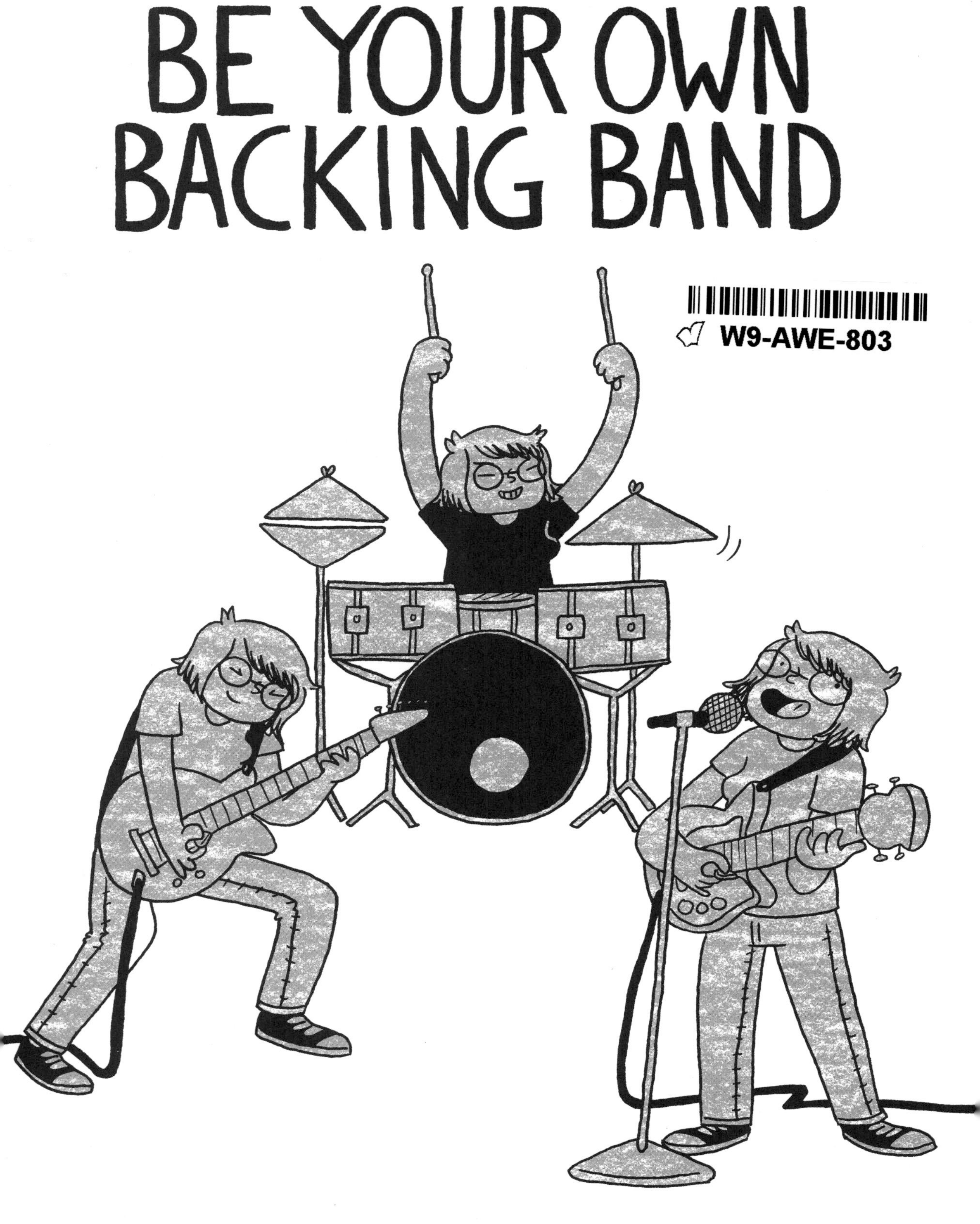

www.lizprincepower.com

Published by:

Silver Sprocket
1057 Valencia Street
San Francisco, CA 94110

www.silversprocket.net

ISBN: 978-1-945509-06-3
SILVER #70

First printing, Spring 2017
Printed in the USA

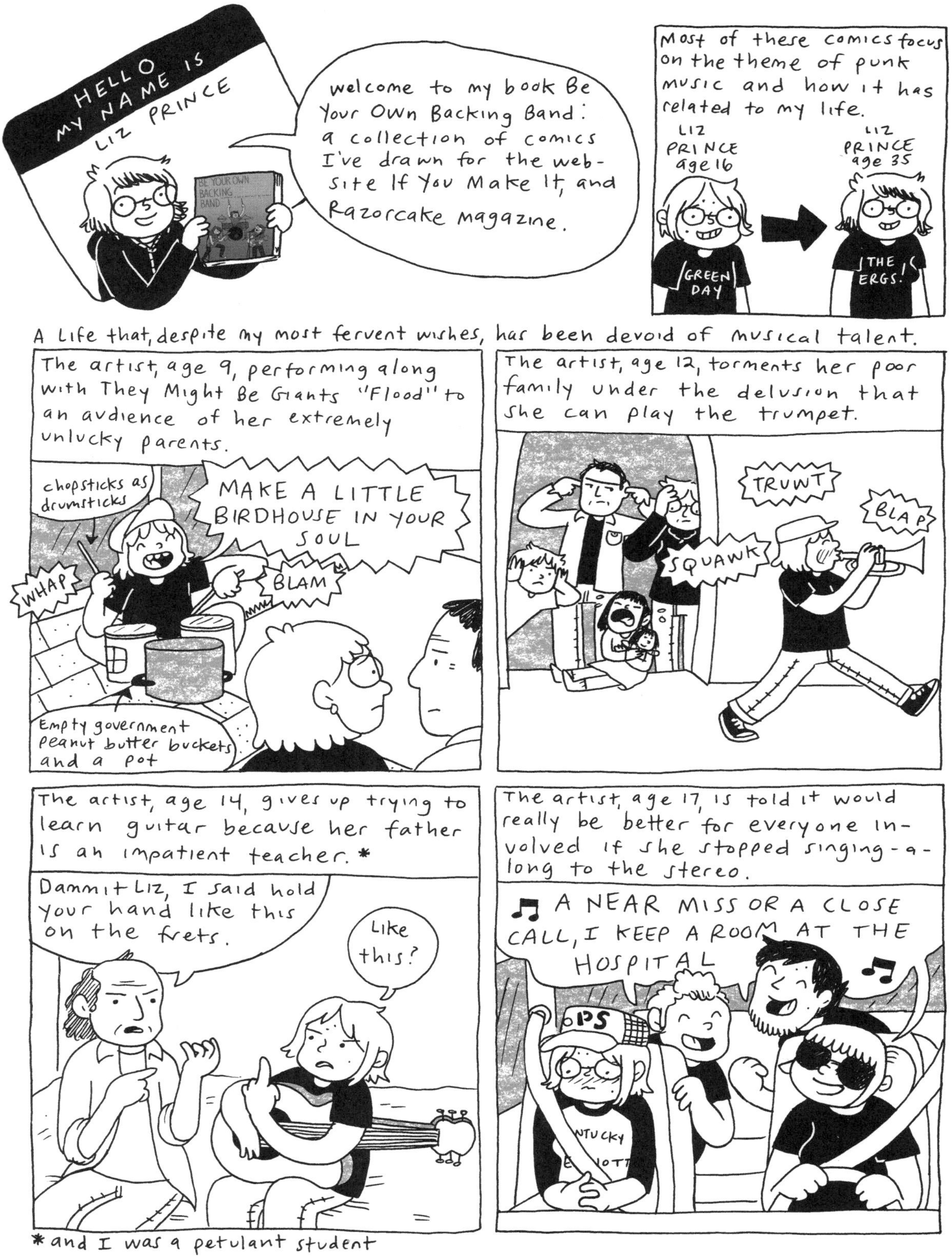
HELLO MY NAME IS LIZ PRINCE
BE YOUR OWN BACKING BAND
welcome to my book Be Your Own Backing Band: a collection of comics I've drawn for the web-site If You Make It, and Razorcake magazine.
Most of these comics focus on the theme of punk music and how it has related to my life.
LIZ PRINCE age 16
GREEN DAY
LIZ PRINCE age 35
THE ERGS!
A Life that, despite my most fervent wishes, has been devoid of musical talent.
The artist, age 9, performing along with They Might Be Giants "Flood" to an audience of her extremely unlucky parents.
chopsticks as drumsticks
MAKE A LITTLE BIRDHOUSE IN YOUR SOUL
WHAP
BLAM
Empty government peanut butter buckets and a pot
The artist, age 12, torments her poor family under the delusion that she can play the trumpet.
TRUWT
BLAP
SQUAWK
The artist, age 14, gives up trying to learn guitar because her father is an impatient teacher.*
Dammit Liz, I said hold your hand like this on the frets.
Like this?
*and I was a petulant student
The artist, age 17, is told it would really be better for everyone involved if she stopped singing-a-long to the stereo.
A NEAR MISS OR A CLOSE CALL, I KEEP A ROOM AT THE HOSPITAL
PS

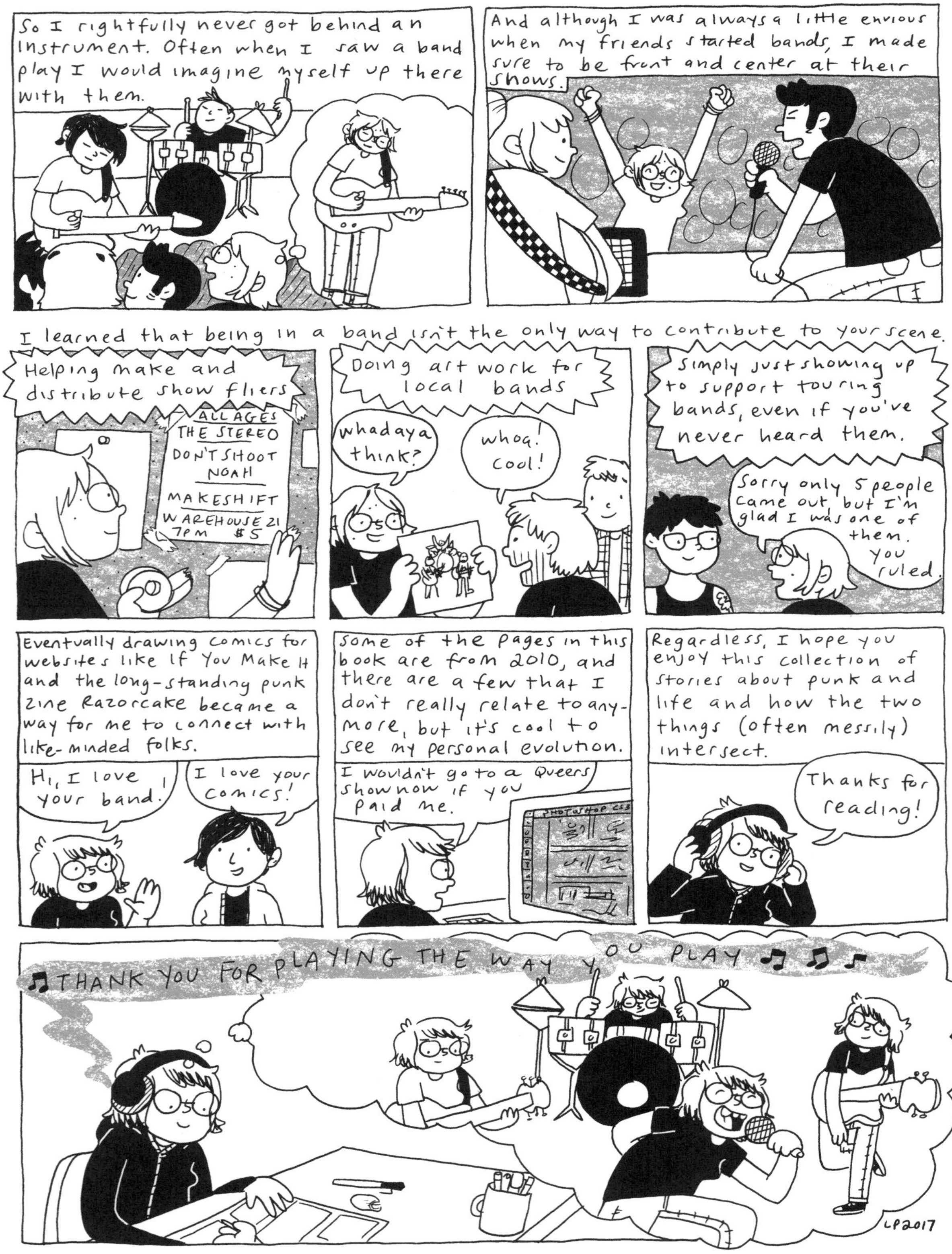
So I rightfully never got behind an instrument. Often when I saw a band play I would imagine myself up there with them.
And although I was always a little envious when my friends started bands, I made sure to be front and center at their shows.
I learned that being in a band isn't the only way to contribute to your scene.
Helping make and distribute show fliers
ALL AGES
THE STEREO
DON'T SHOOT NOAH
MAKESHIFT
WAREHOUSE 21
7PM $5
Doing art work for local bands
whadaya think?
whoa! cool!
Simply just showing up to support touring bands, even if you've never heard them.
Sorry only 5 people came out, but I'm glad I was one of them. You ruled.
Eventually drawing comics for websites like If You Make It and the long-standing punk zine Razorcake became a way for me to connect with like-minded folks.
Hi, I love your band!
I love your comics!
Some of the pages in this book are from 2010, and there are a few that I don't really relate to anymore, but it's cool to see my personal evolution.
I wouldn't go to a Queers show now if you paid me.
Regardless, I hope you enjoy this collection of stories about punk and life and how the two things (often messily) intersect.
Thanks for reading!
♫ THANK YOU FOR PLAYING THE WAY YOU PLAY ♫ ♫ ♪
LP2017

If You Make It was/is a Brooklyn-based music website that I started in 2006. In the beginning it was just a Wordpress blog with live videos of bands that I had shot on my trusty camera. Over the years, I added more sections, rebuilt the site a hundred times, and tried my best to let others help me. IYMI is home to the Pink Couch Sessions, where I invited around 120 different bands to come over to my house and record music on my big ugly pink Ikea couch. The site also is also home to music videos, over 100 free records, band interviews, and a single podcast.

In 2008, while on tour with my band Halo Fauna, I stumbled upon Liz's books "Will You Still Love Me If I Wet The Bed?" and "Delayed Replays" at the Frisby House in Baltimore, MD. I loved them both instantly and in early 2009, I reached out to see if she'd be interested in contributing to a new comics section. She said yes, and soon after we launched with "Punk Rock is Ruining My Teeth". I am so grateful for Liz's contributions and how she shaped If You Make It as something more than a music site. Her work helped convince the other future artists (Ramsey Beyer, Jim Kettner, Sally Madden and Mikey Heller) that this was something real. Over the years, the site grew to encompass around 40 comics about live, love and the pursuit of good music.

-Dave Garwacke, If You Make It

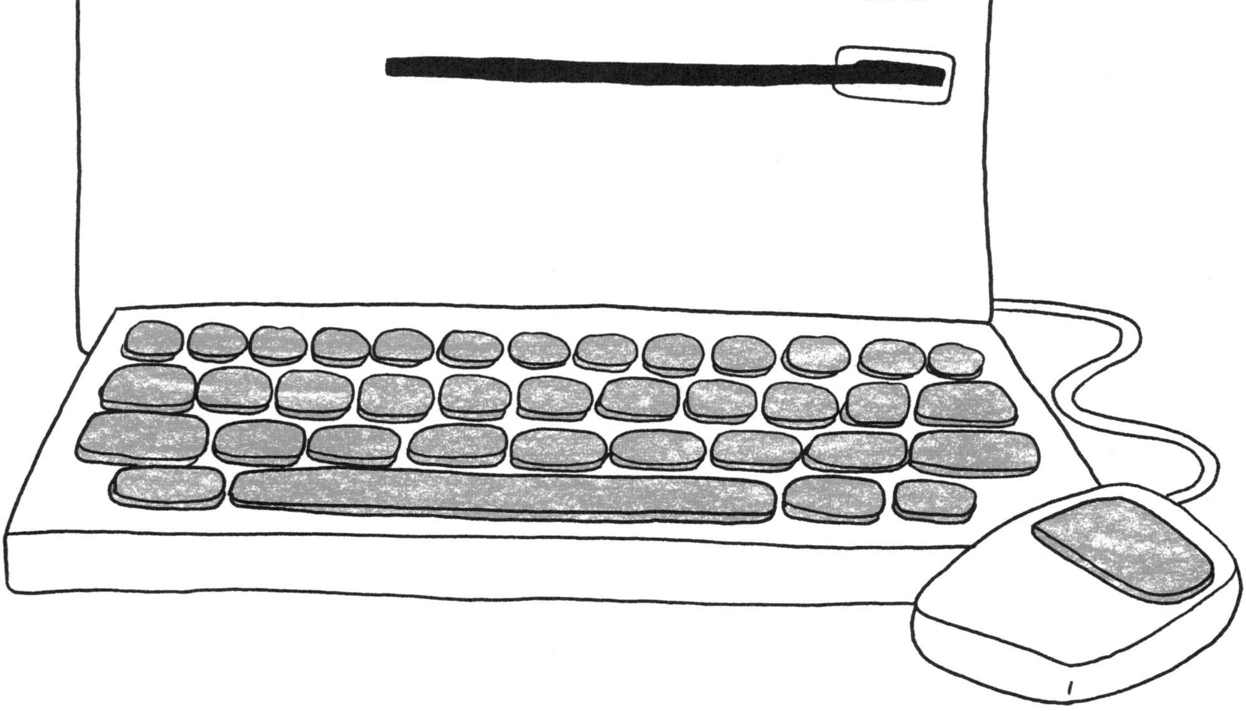

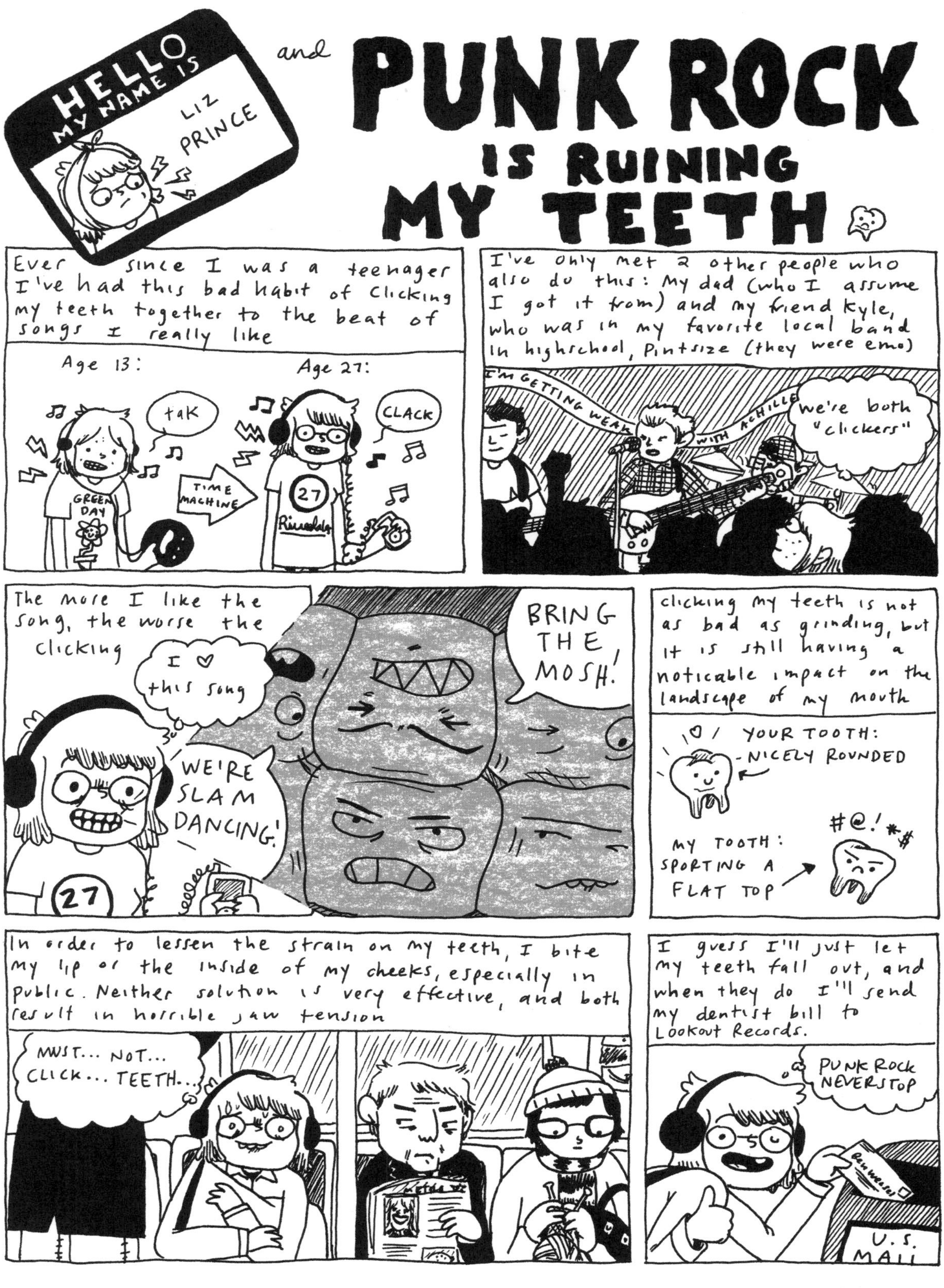
HELLO MY NAME IS
LIZ PRINCE
and
PUNK ROCK IS RUINING MY TEETH
Ever since I was a teenager I've had this bad habit of clicking my teeth together to the beat of songs I really like
Age 13:
tak
GREEN DAY
TIME MACHINE
Age 27:
CLACK
27
I've only met 2 other people who also do this: My dad (who I assume I got it from) and my friend Kyle, who was in my favorite local band in highschool, Pintsize (they were emo)
I'M GETTING WEAK WITH ACHILLES
We're both "clickers"
The more I like the song, the worse the clicking
I ♡ this song
WE'RE SLAM DANCING!
BRING THE MOSH!
27
clicking my teeth is not as bad as grinding, but it is still having a noticable impact on the landscape of my mouth
YOUR TOOTH: -NICELY ROUNDED
MY TOOTH: SPORTING A FLAT TOP
#@!*$
In order to lessen the strain on my teeth, I bite my lip or the inside of my cheeks, especially in public. Neither solution is very effective, and both result in horrible jaw tension
MUST... NOT... CLICK... TEETH...
I guess I'll just let my teeth fall out, and when they do I'll send my dentist bill to Lookout Records.
PUNK ROCK NEVERSTOP
U.S. MAIL

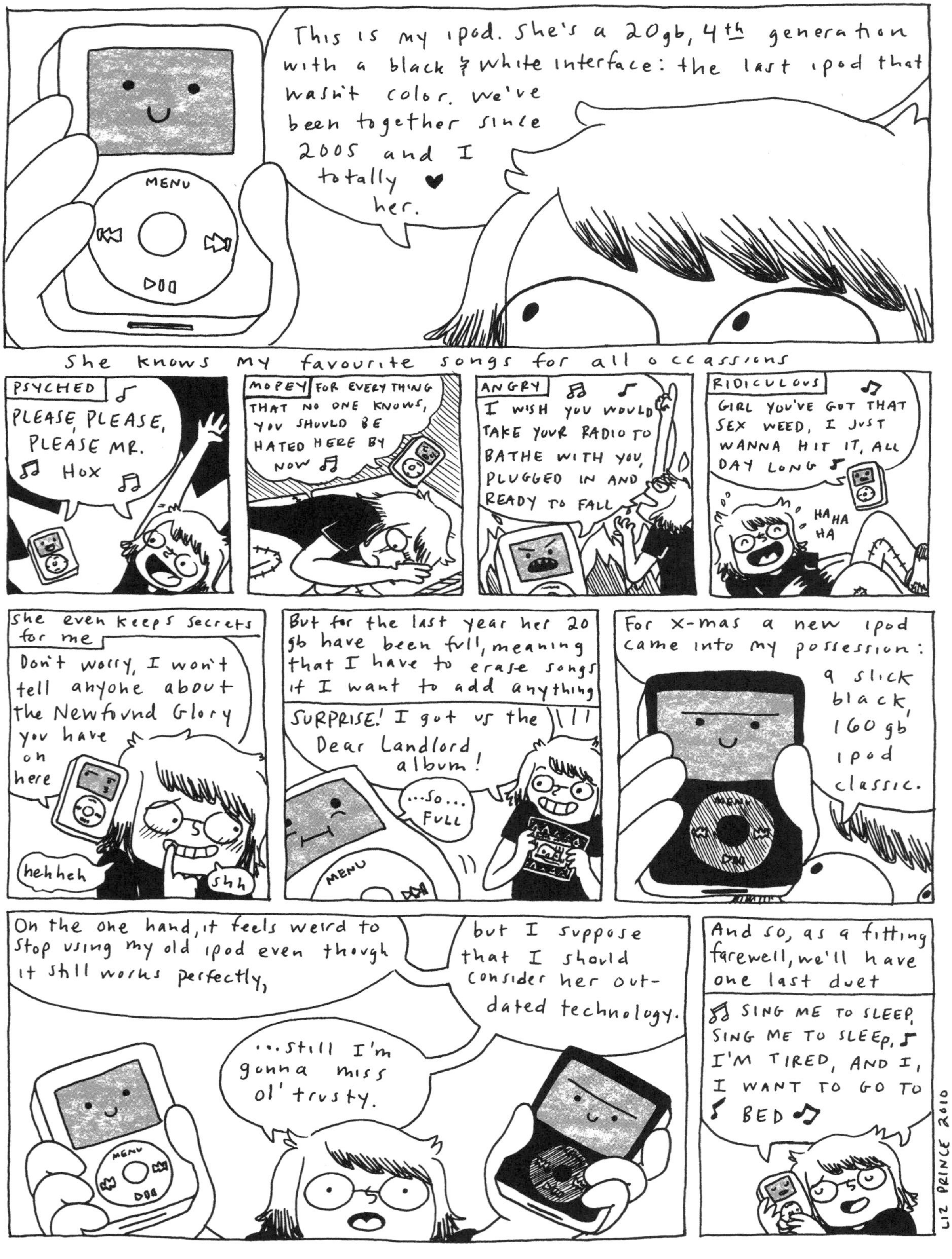
This is my ipod. She's a 20gb, 4th generation with a black & white interface: the last ipod that wasn't color. We've been together since 2005 and I totally ♥ her.
MENU
She knows my favourite songs for all occassions
PSYCHED
PLEASE, PLEASE, PLEASE MR. HOX
MOPEY
FOR EVERYTHING THAT NO ONE KNOWS, YOU SHOULD BE HATED HERE BY NOW
ANGRY
I WISH YOU WOULD TAKE YOUR RADIO TO BATHE WITH YOU, PLUGGED IN AND READY TO FALL
RIDICULOUS
GIRL YOU'VE GOT THAT SEX WEED, I JUST WANNA HIT IT, ALL DAY LONG
HA HA HA
she even keeps secrets for me
Don't worry, I won't tell anyone about the Newfound Glory you have on here
hehheh
shh
But for the last year her 20 gb have been full, meaning that I have to erase songs if I want to add anything
SURPRISE! I got us the Dear Landlord album!
...so... FULL
MENU
For X-mas a new ipod came into my possession:
a slick black, 160 gb ipod classic.
On the one hand, it feels weird to stop using my old ipod even though it still works perfectly,
but I suppose that I should consider her out-dated technology.
...still I'm gonna miss ol' trusty.
MENU
And so, as a fitting farewell, we'll have one last duet
SING ME TO SLEEP, SING ME TO SLEEP, I'M TIRED, AND I, I WANT TO GO TO BED
LIZ PRINCE 2010

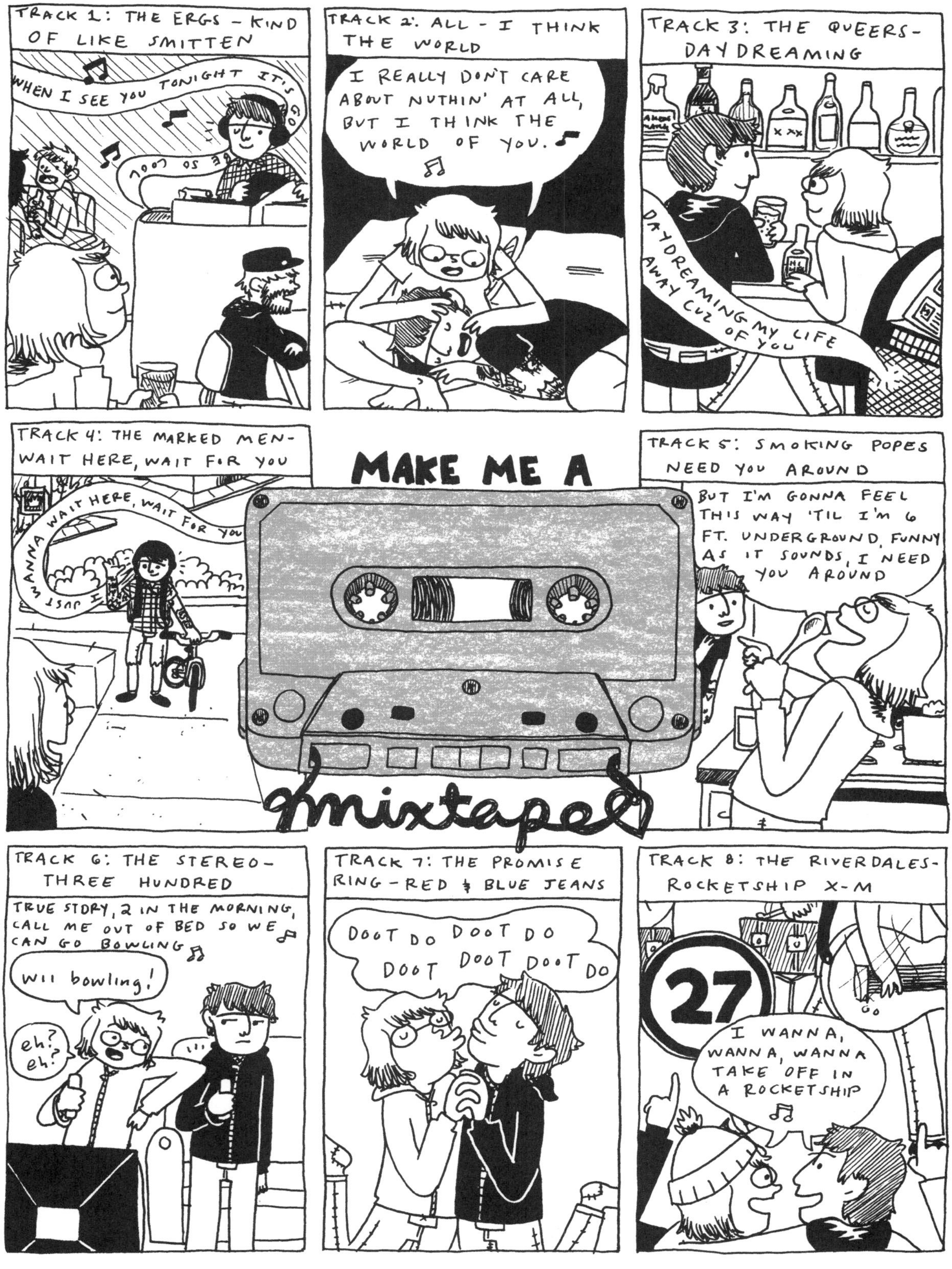
TRACK 1: THE ERGS - KIND OF LIKE SMITTEN
WHEN I SEE YOU TONIGHT IT'S GO
E SO COOL
TRACK 2: ALL - I THINK THE WORLD
I REALLY DON'T CARE ABOUT NUTHIN' AT ALL, BUT I THINK THE WORLD OF YOU.
TRACK 3: THE QUEERS - DAYDREAMING
DAYDREAMING MY LIFE AWAY CUZ OF YOU
TRACK 4: THE MARKED MEN - WAIT HERE, WAIT FOR YOU
I JUST WANNA WAIT HERE, WAIT FOR YOU
MAKE ME A
mixtape
TRACK 5: SMOKING POPES NEED YOU AROUND
BUT I'M GONNA FEEL THIS WAY 'TIL I'M 6 FT. UNDERGROUND, FUNNY AS IT SOUNDS, I NEED YOU AROUND
TRACK 6: THE STEREO - THREE HUNDRED
TRUE STORY, 2 IN THE MORNING, CALL ME OUT OF BED SO WE CAN GO BOWLING
Wii bowling!
eh? eh?
TRACK 7: THE PROMISE RING - RED & BLUE JEANS
DOOT DO DOOT DO DOOT DOOT DOOT DO
TRACK 8: THE RIVERDALES - ROCKETSHIP X-M
27
I WANNA, WANNA, WANNA TAKE OFF IN A ROCKETSHIP

LIZ PRINCE'S DINNER THEATRE PROUDLY PRESENTS

Cooking with The Methadones

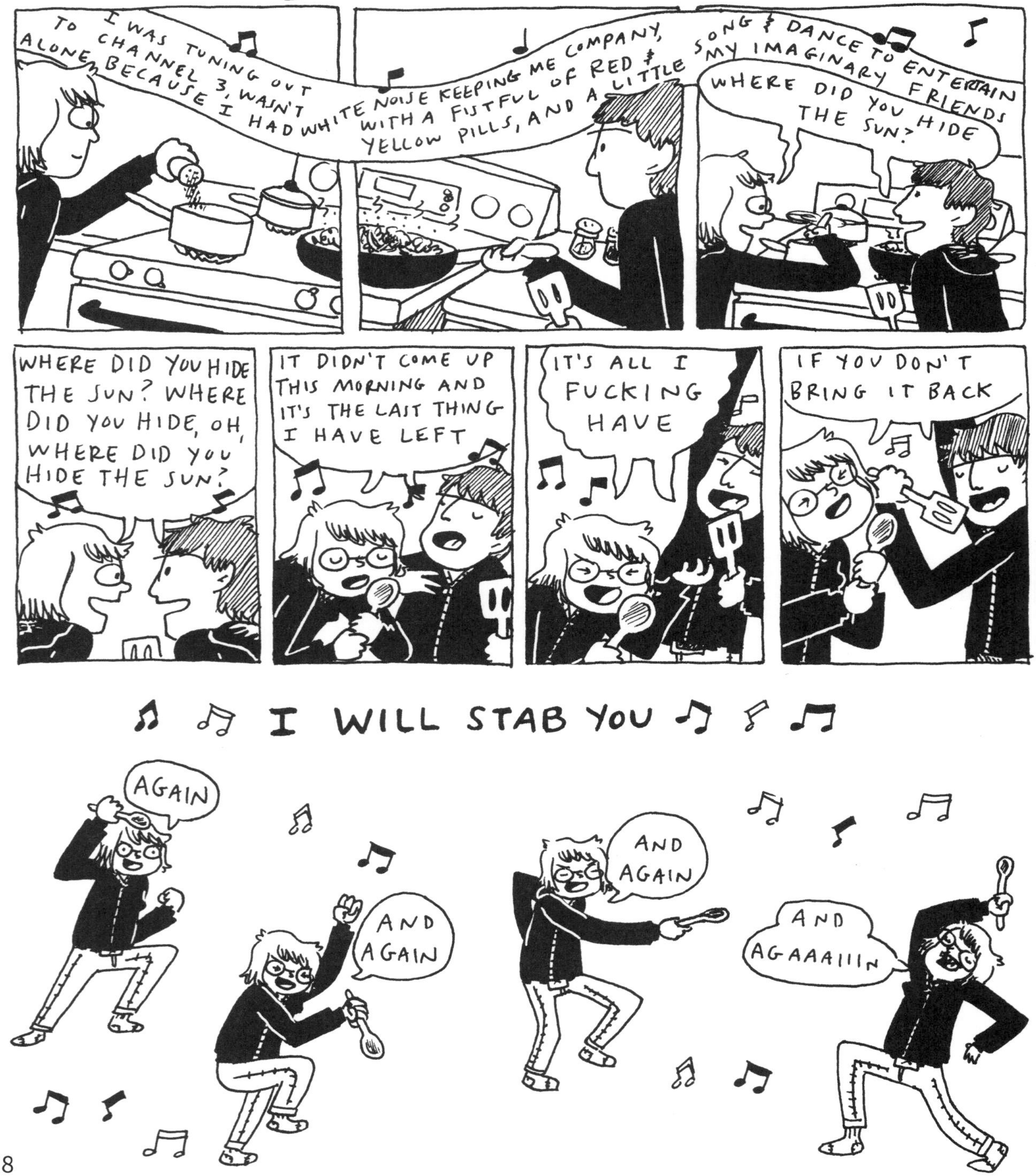
I WAS TUNING OUT TO CHANNEL 3, WASN'T ALONE BECAUSE I HAD WHITE NOISE KEEPING ME COMPANY, WITH A FISTFUL OF RED & YELLOW PILLS, AND A LITTLE SONG & DANCE TO ENTERTAIN MY IMAGINARY FRIENDS
WHERE DID YOU HIDE THE SUN?
WHERE DID YOU HIDE THE SUN? WHERE DID YOU HIDE, OH, WHERE DID YOU HIDE THE SUN?
IT DIDN'T COME UP THIS MORNING AND IT'S THE LAST THING I HAVE LEFT
IT'S ALL I FUCKING HAVE
IF YOU DON'T BRING IT BACK
I WILL STAB YOU
AGAIN
AND AGAIN
AND AGAIN
AND AGAAAIIIN

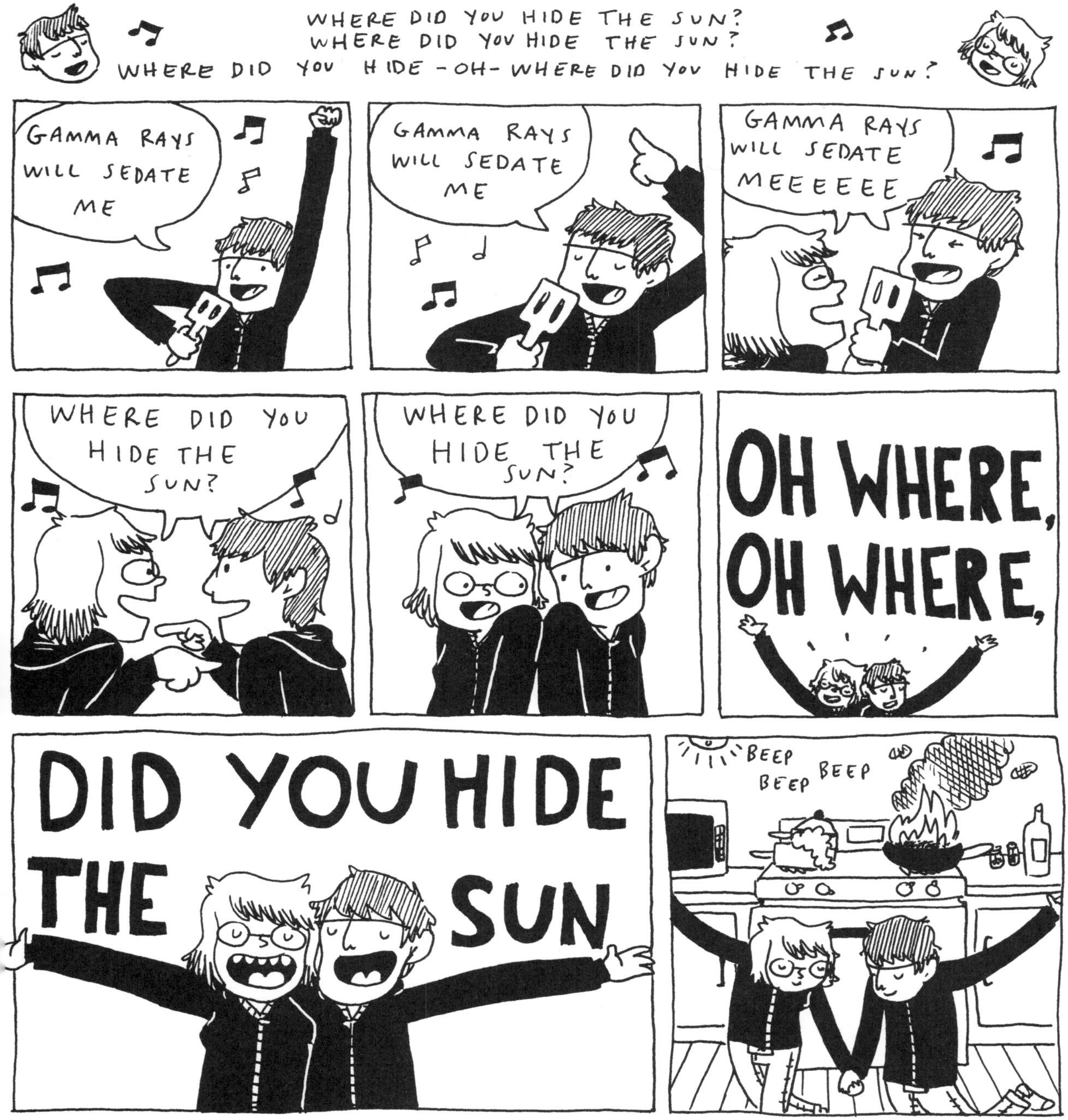
WHERE DID YOU HIDE THE SUN?
WHERE DID YOU HIDE THE SUN?
WHERE DID YOU HIDE -OH- WHERE DID YOU HIDE THE SUN?
GAMMA RAYS WILL SEDATE ME
GAMMA RAYS WILL SEDATE ME
GAMMA RAYS WILL SEDATE MEEEEEE
WHERE DID YOU HIDE THE SUN?
WHERE DID YOU HIDE THE SUN?
OH WHERE, OH WHERE,
DID YOU HIDE THE SUN
BEEP
BEEP
BEEP

comic drawn by Liz Prince, 2010.

"Where Did You Hide The Sun" by The Methadones, lyrics used without permission, but please don't sue me. Thanks.

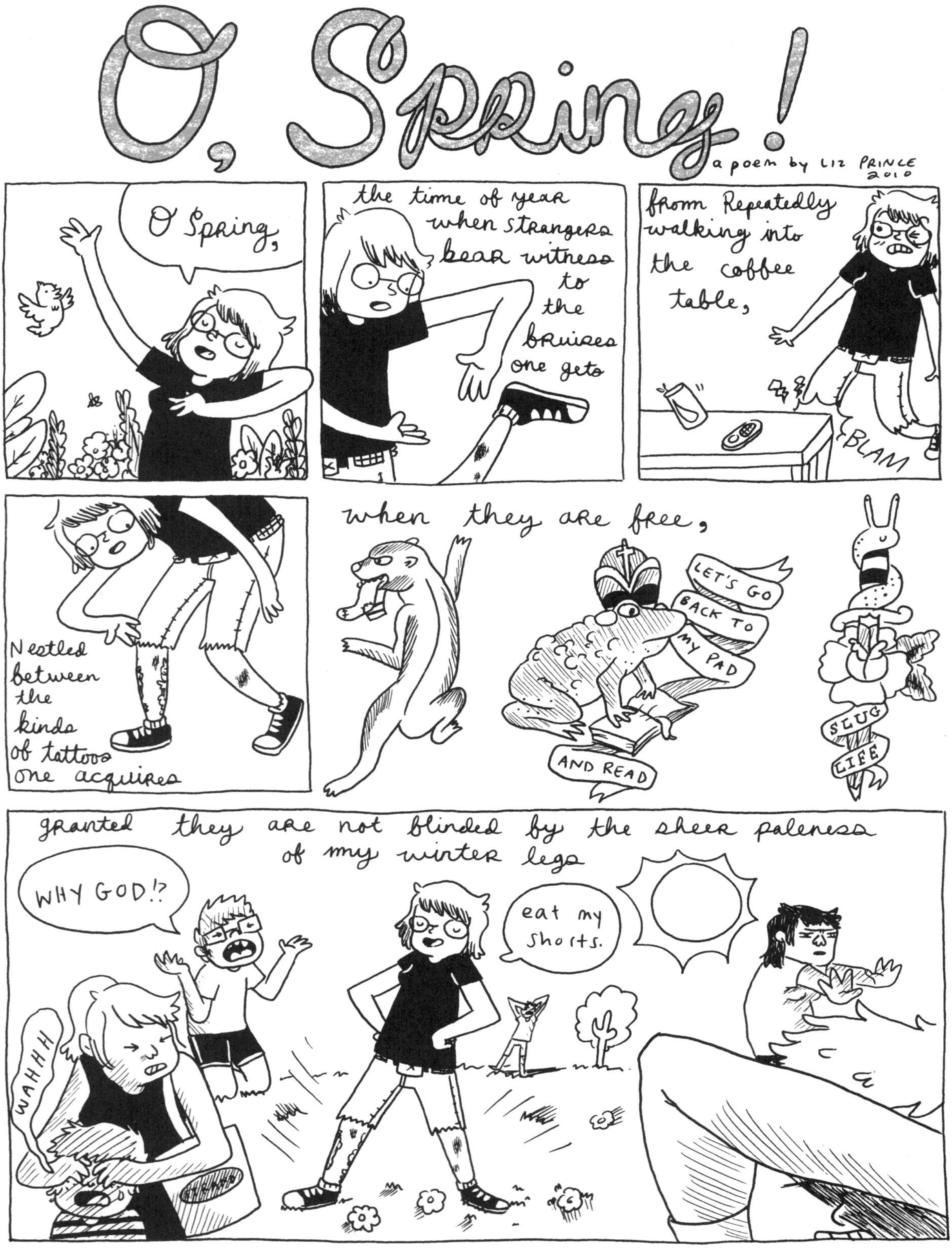
O, Spring!
a poem by LIZ PRINCE 2010
O Spring,
the time of year when strangers bear witness to the bruises one gets
from repeatedly walking into the coffee table,
BLAM
Nestled between the kinds of tattoos one acquires
when they are free,
LET'S GO BACK TO MY PAD AND READ
SLUG LIFE
granted they are not blinded by the sheer paleness of my winter legs
WHY GOD!?
WAHHH
eat my shorts.

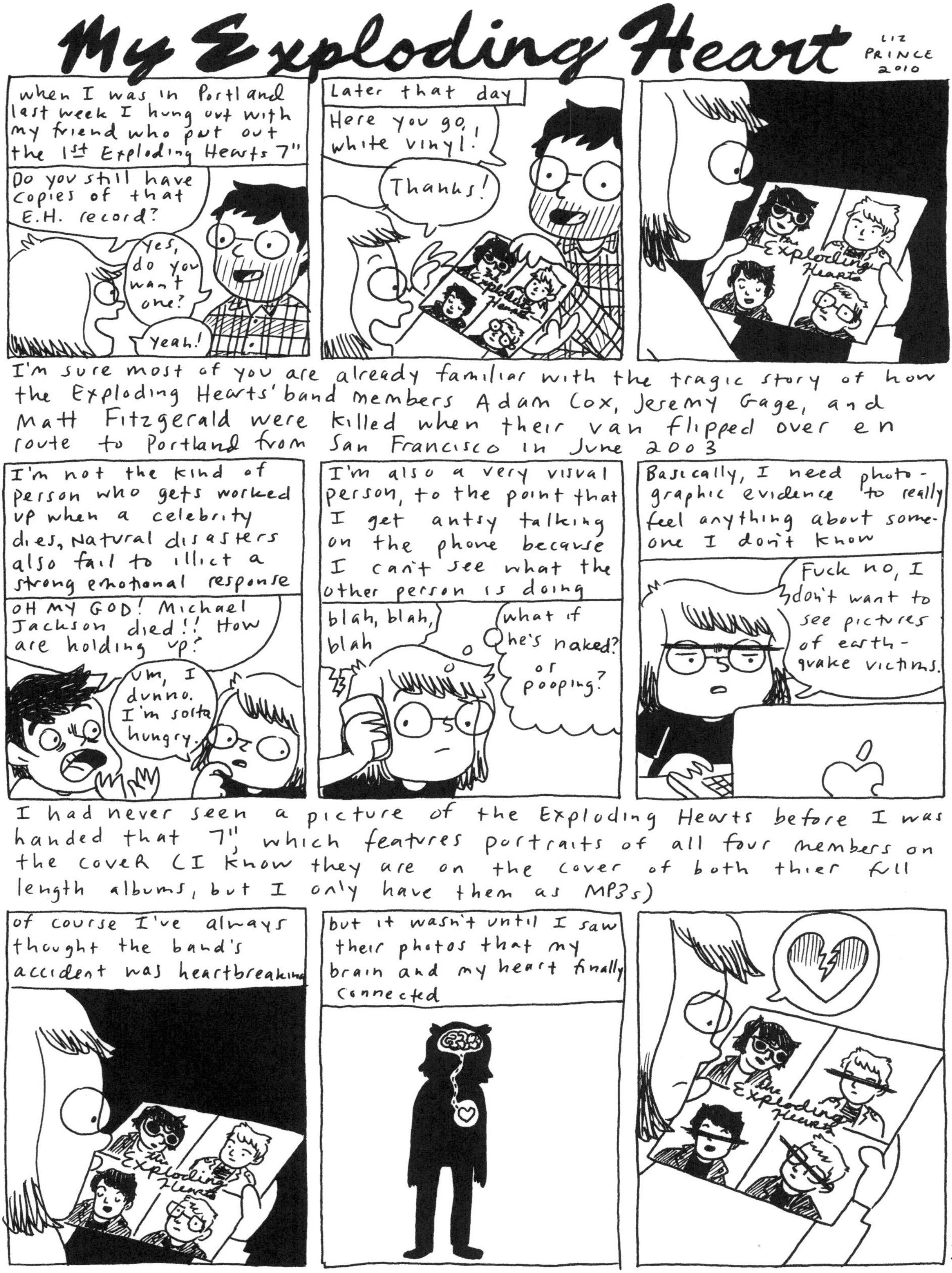
My Exploding Heart
LIZ PRINCE 2010
when I was in Portland last week I hung out with my friend who put out the 1st Exploding Hearts 7"
Do you still have copies of that E.H. record?
Yes, do you want one?
Yeah!
Later that day
Here you go, white vinyl!
Thanks!
The Exploding Hearts
I'm sure most of you are already familiar with the tragic story of how the Exploding Hearts' band members Adam Cox, Jeremy Gage, and Matt Fitzgerald were killed when their van flipped over en route to Portland from San Francisco in June 2003
I'm not the kind of person who gets worked up when a celebrity dies, Natural disasters also fail to illict a strong emotional response
OH MY GOD! Michael Jackson died!! How are holding up?
Um, I dunno. I'm sorta hungry.
I'm also a very visual person, to the point that I get antsy talking on the phone because I can't see what the other person is doing
blah, blah, blah
what if he's naked? or pooping?
Basically, I need photographic evidence to really feel anything about someone I don't know
Fuck no, I don't want to see pictures of earthquake victims.
I had never seen a picture of the Exploding Hearts before I was handed that 7", which features portraits of all four members on the cover (I know they are on the cover of both thier full length albums, but I only have them as MP3s)
of course I've always thought the band's accident was heartbreaking
but it wasn't until I saw their photos that my brain and my heart finally connected

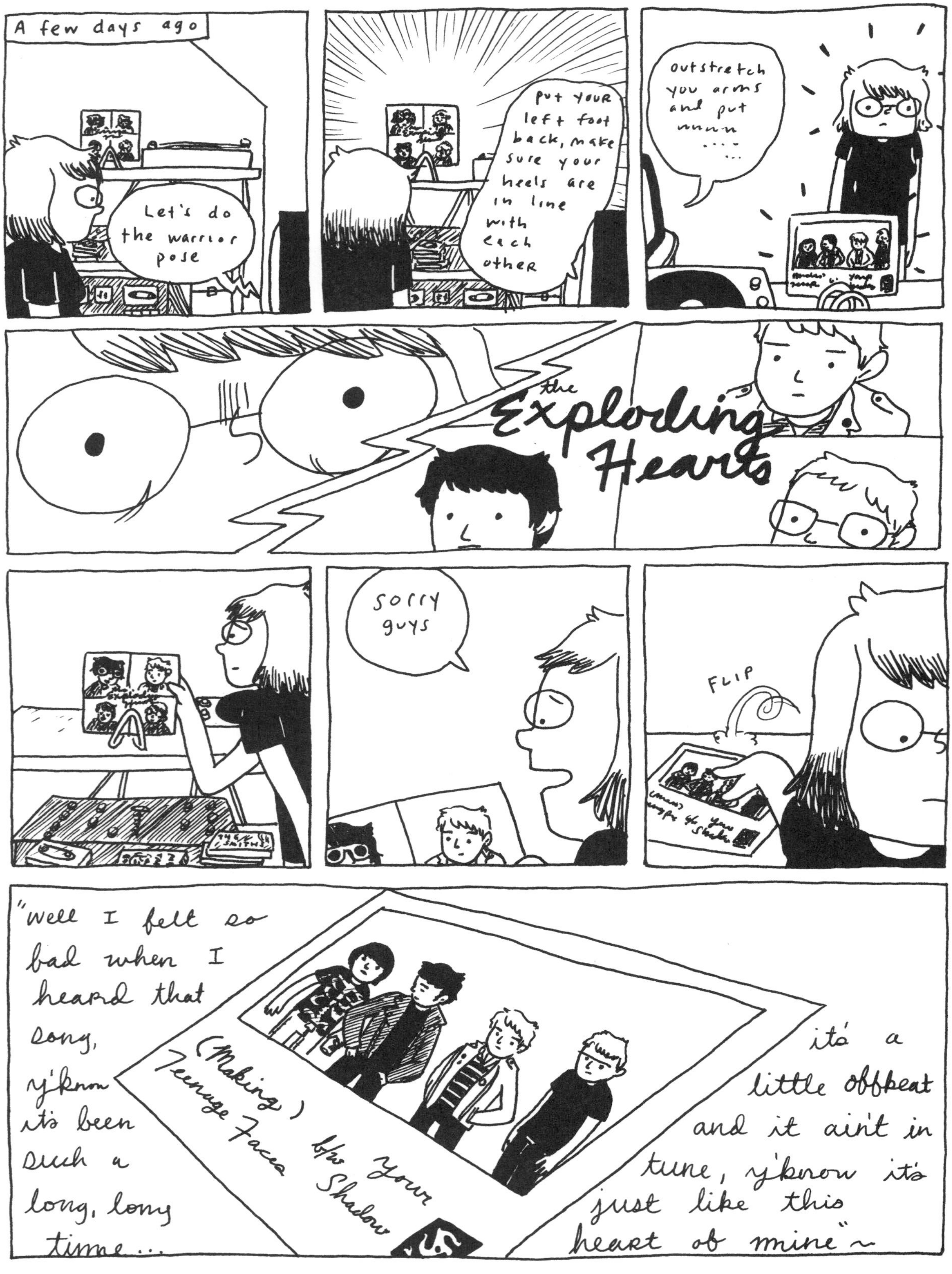
A few days ago
Let's do the warrior pose
put your left foot back, make sure your heels are in line with each other
outstretch you arms and put nnnn ....
the Exploding Hearts
sorry guys
FLIP
"Well I felt so bad when I heard that song, y'know it's been such a long, long time...
(Making) Teenage Faces b/w Your Shadow
it's a little offbeat and it ain't in tune, y'know it's just like this heart of mine"~

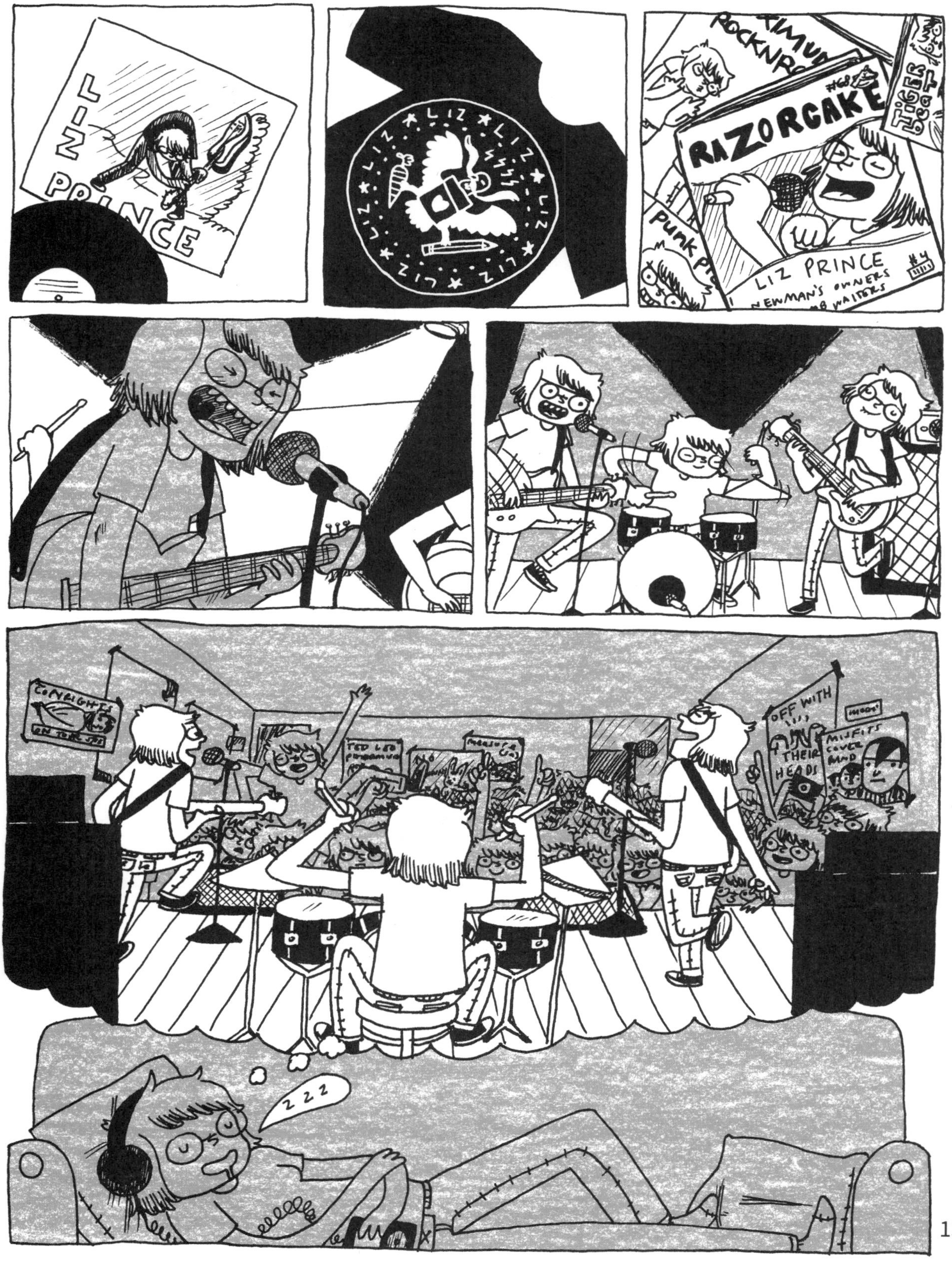
LIZ PRINCE
LIZ ★ LIZ ★ LIZ ★ LIZ ★ LIZ ★ LIZ ★ LIZ ★ LIZ
RAZORCAKE
#68
LIZ PRINCE
NEWMAN'S OWNERS
#4
COPYRIGHTS
OFF WITH THEIR HEADS
MISFITS COVER BAND
ZZZ

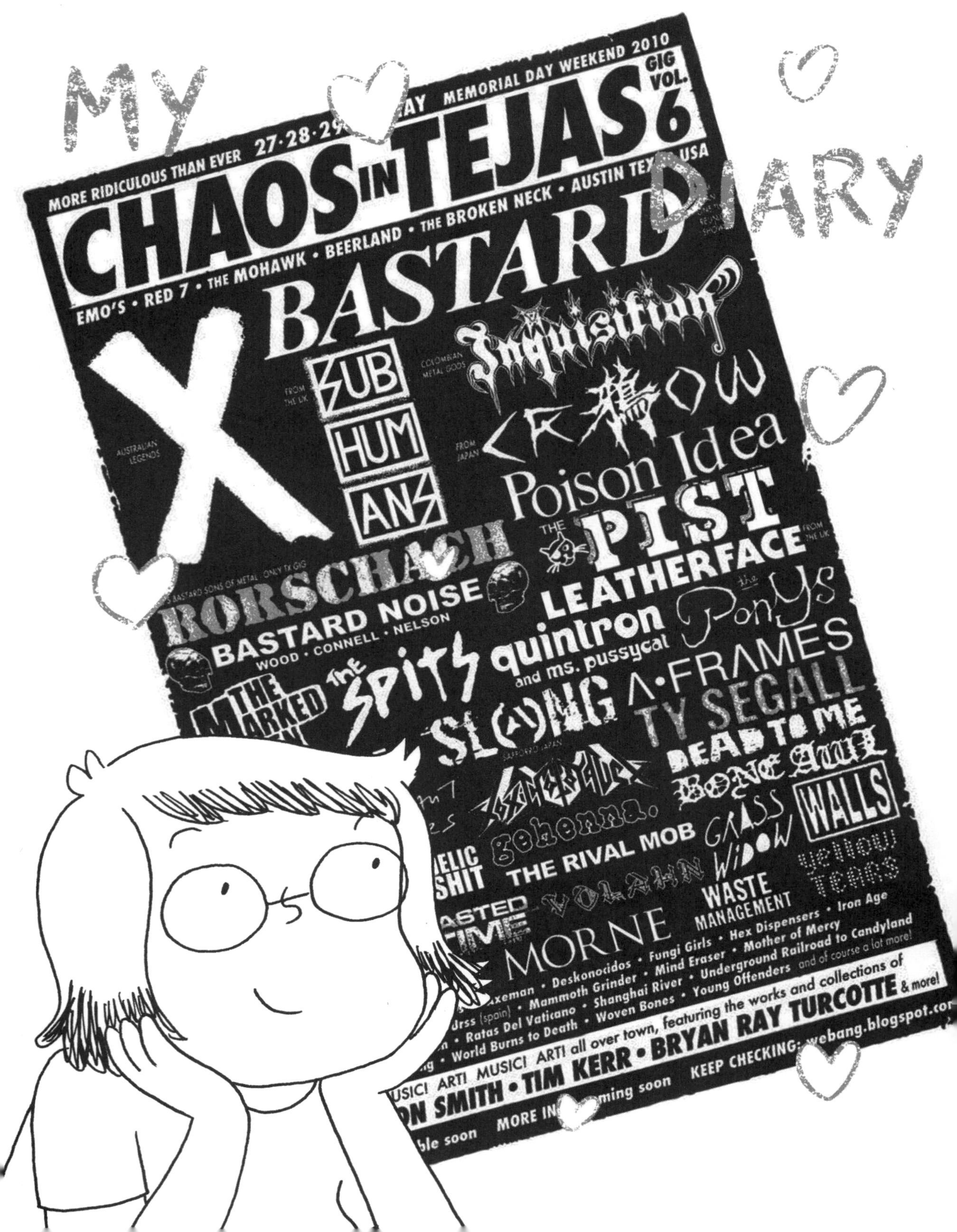
MY DIARY
MEMORIAL DAY WEEKEND 2010
GIG VOL. 6
MORE RIDICULOUS THAN EVER
CHAOS IN TEJAS
THE BROKEN NECK • AUSTIN TEX
EMO'S • RED 7 • THE MOHAWK • BEERLAND
X
AUSTRALIAN LEGENDS
BASTARD
Inquisition
COLOMBIAN METAL GODS
FROM THE UK
SUB HUM ANS
FROM JAPAN
Poison Idea
THE PIST
FROM THE UK
RORSCHACH
LEATHERFACE
BASTARD NOISE
WOOD • CONNELL • NELSON
the Ponys
quintron and ms. pussycal
the SPITS
A-FRAMES
TY SEGALL
DEAD TO ME
BONE AWL
WALLS
gehenna.
THE RIVAL MOB
GRASS WIDOW
THE RIVAL MOB
WASTE MANAGEMENT
MORNE
Hex Dispensers • Iron Age
Deskonocidos • Fungi Girls • Mother of Mercy
Mammoth Grinder • Mind Eraser • Underground Railroad to Candyland
Shanghai River • Young Offenders and of course a lot more!
Ratas Del Vaticano • Woven Bones
World Burns to Death
all over town, featuring the works and collections of
TIM KERR • BRYAN RAY TURCOTTE & more!
KEEP CHECKING: webang.blogspot.com
MORE IN coming soon

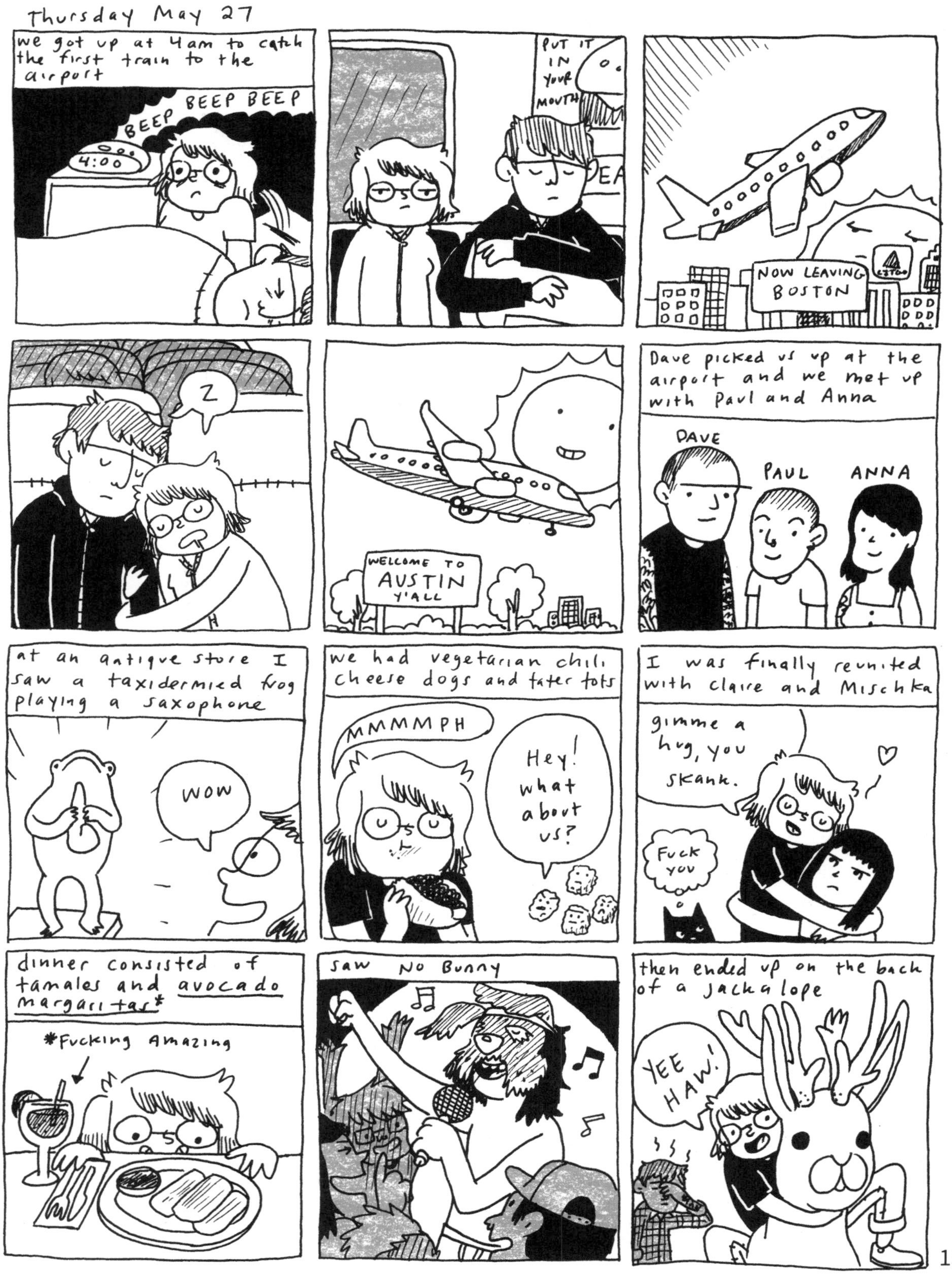
Thursday May 27
we got up at 4am to catch the first train to the airport
BEEP BEEP BEEP
4:00
PUT IT IN YOUR MOUTH
EA
NOW LEAVING BOSTON
Z
WELCOME TO AUSTIN Y'ALL
Dave picked us up at the airport and we met up with Paul and Anna
DAVE
PAUL
ANNA
at an antique store I saw a taxidermied frog playing a saxophone
WOW
we had vegetarian chili cheese dogs and tater tots
MMMMPH
Hey! what about us?
I was finally reunited with claire and Mischka
gimme a hug, you skank.
Fuck you
dinner consisted of tamales and avocado margaritas*
*Fucking Amazing
saw No Bunny
then ended up on the back of a jackalope
YEE HAW!

Friday May 28

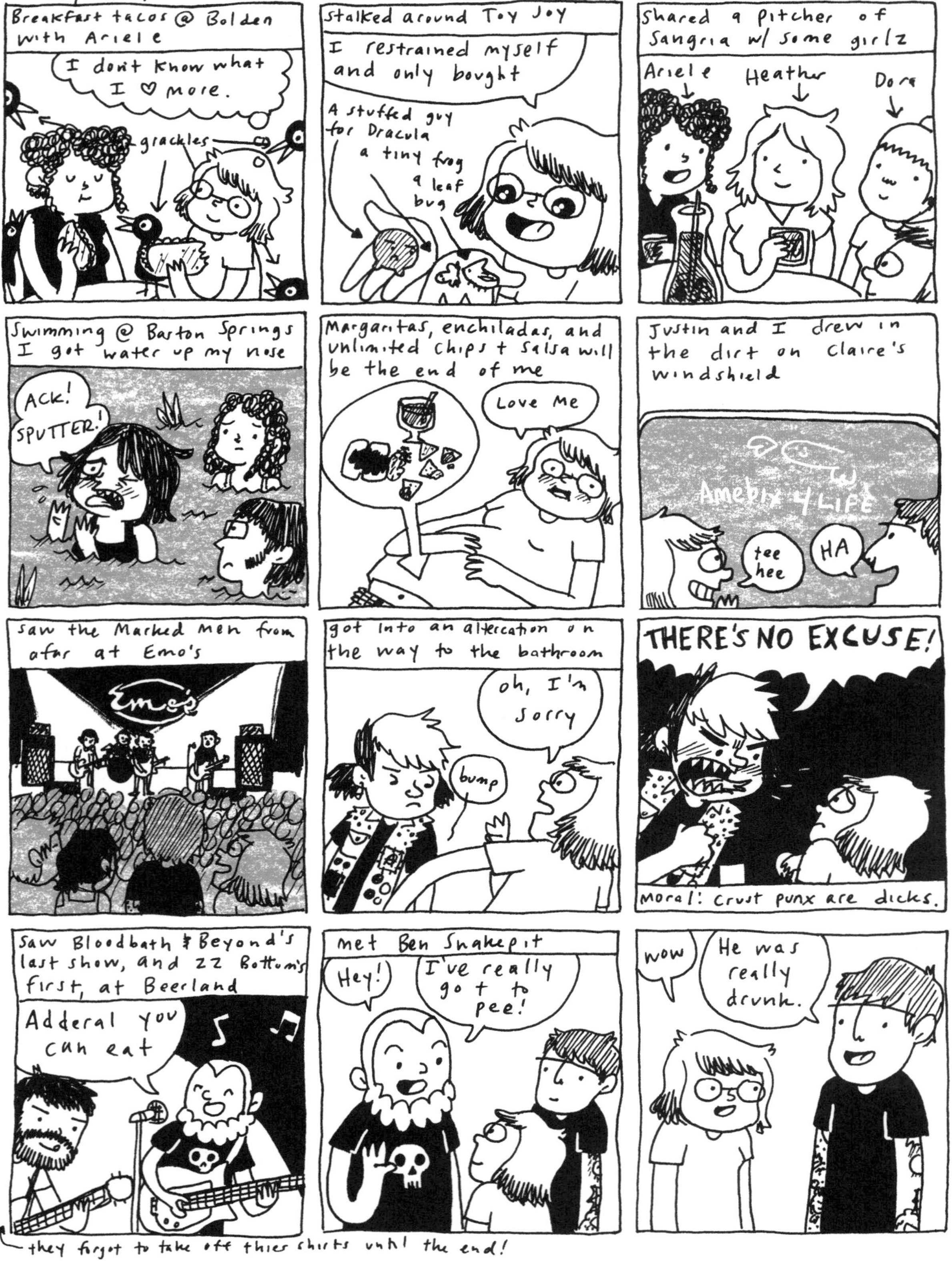
Breakfast tacos @ Bolden with Ariele
I don't know what I ♡ more.
grackles
stalked around Toy Joy
I restrained myself and only bought
A stuffed guy for Dracula
a tiny frog
a leaf bug
Shared a pitcher of Sangria w/ some girlz
Ariele
Heather
Dora
Swimming @ Barton Springs I got water up my nose
ACK! SPUTTER!
Margaritas, enchiladas, and unlimited chips + salsa will be the end of me
Love Me
Justin and I drew in the dirt on Claire's windshield
Amebix 4 LIFE
tee hee
HA
saw the Marked Men from afar at Emo's
Emo's
got into an altercation on the way to the bathroom
oh, I'm sorry
bump
THERE'S NO EXCUSE!
Moral: crust punx are dicks.
Saw Bloodbath & Beyond's last show, and ZZ Bottom's first, at Beerland
Adderal you can eat
met Ben Snakepit
Hey!
I've really got to pee!
wow
He was really drunk.
they forgot to take off thier shirts until the end!

Saturday May 29

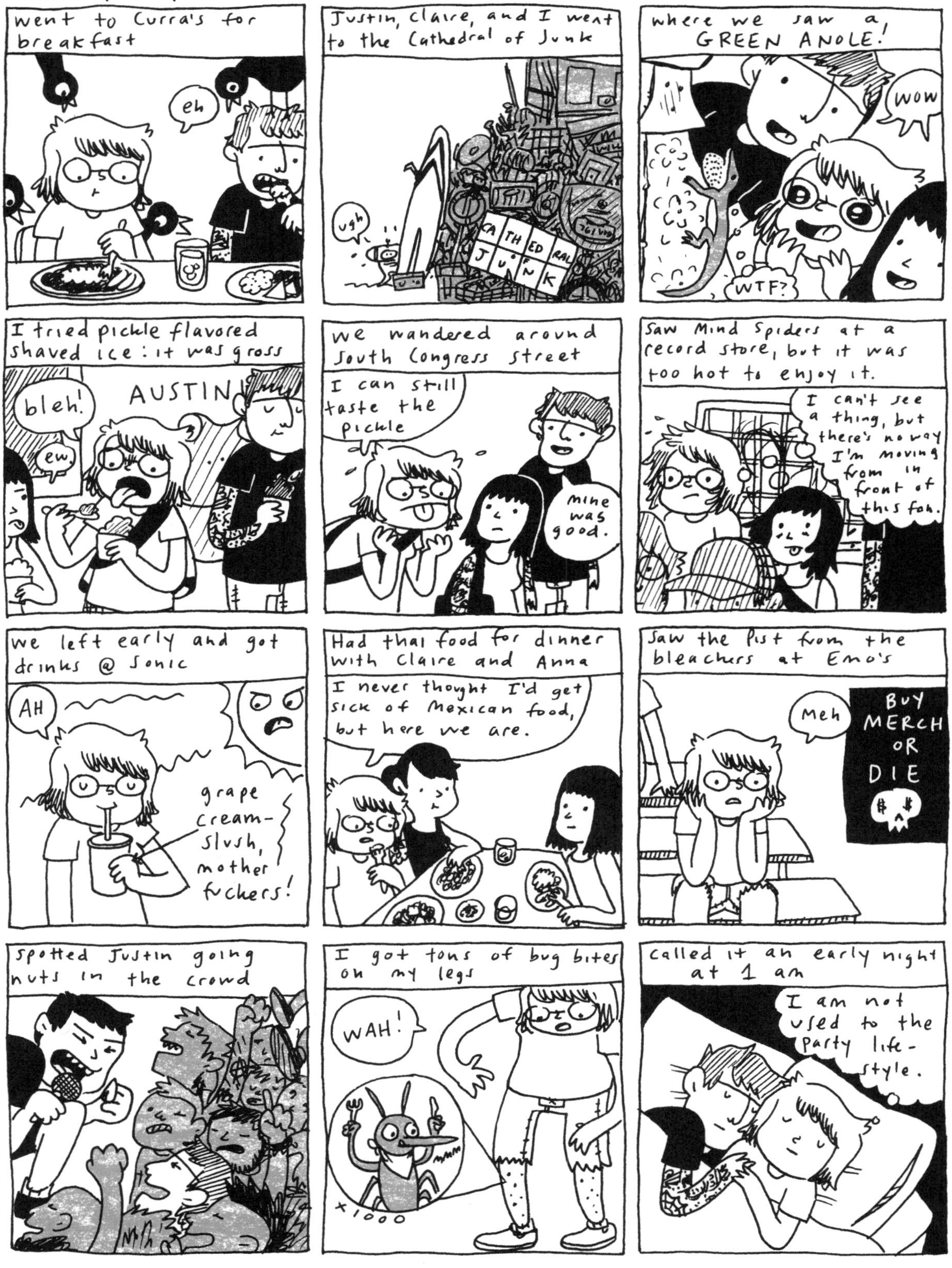
went to Curra's for breakfast
eh
Justin, Claire, and I went to the Cathedral of Junk
ugh
CATHEDRAL JUNK
where we saw a, GREEN ANOLE!
WOW
WTF?
I tried pickle flavored shaved ice: it was gross
bleh!
AUSTIN
ew.
we wandered around South Congress street
I can still taste the pickle
mine was good.
Saw Mind Spiders at a record store, but it was too hot to enjoy it.
I can't see a thing, but there's no way I'm moving from in front of this fan.
we left early and got drinks @ Sonic
AH
grape cream-slush, mother fuckers!
Had thai food for dinner with Claire and Anna
I never thought I'd get sick of Mexican food, but here we are.
Saw the Pist from the bleachers at Emo's
Meh
BUY MERCH OR DIE
spotted Justin going nuts in the crowd
I got tons of bug bites on my legs
WAH!
x1000
Called it an early night at 1 am
I am not used to the party life-style.

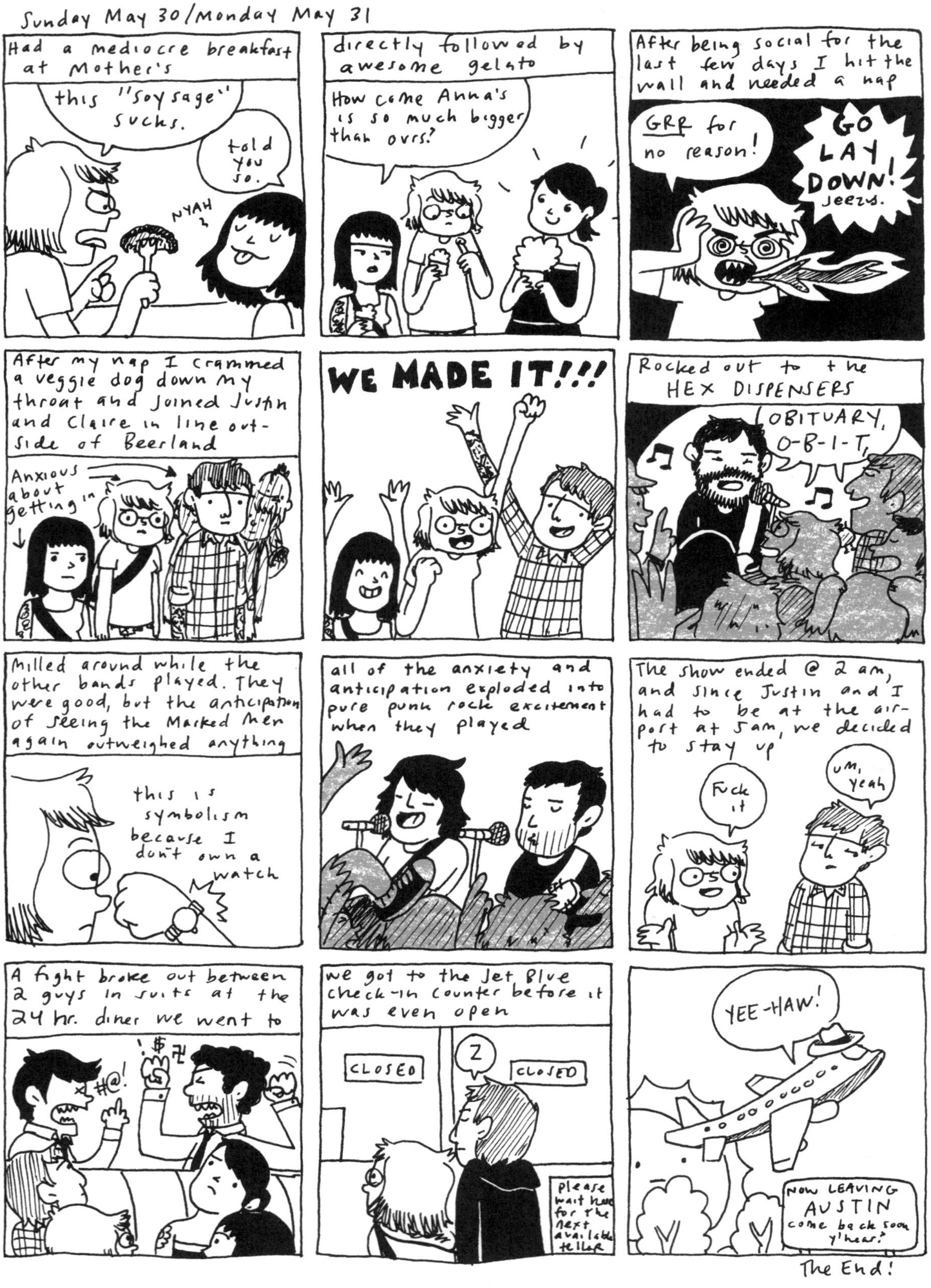
Sunday May 30/Monday May 31
Had a mediocre breakfast at Mother's
this "soysage" sucks.
told you so.
NYAH
directly followed by awesome gelato
How come Anna's is so much bigger than ours?
After being social for the last few days I hit the wall and needed a nap
GRR for no reason!
GO LAY DOWN! Jeezus.
After my nap I crammed a veggie dog down my throat and joined Justin and Claire in line outside of Beerland
Anxious about getting in
WE MADE IT!!!
Rocked out to the HEX DISPENSERS
OBITUARY, O-B-I-T,
Milled around while the other bands played. They were good, but the anticipation of seeing the Marked Men again outweighed anything
this is symbolism because I don't own a watch
all of the anxiety and anticipation exploded into pure punk rock excitement when they played
The show ended @ 2 am, and since Justin and I had to be at the airport at 5am, we decided to stay up
Fuck it
um, yeah
A fight broke out between 2 guys in suits at the 24 hr. diner we went to
#@!
!$
we got to the Jet Blue check-in counter before it was even open
CLOSED
Z
CLOSED
please wait here for the next available teller
YEE-HAW!
NOW LEAVING AUSTIN come back soon y'hear?
The End!

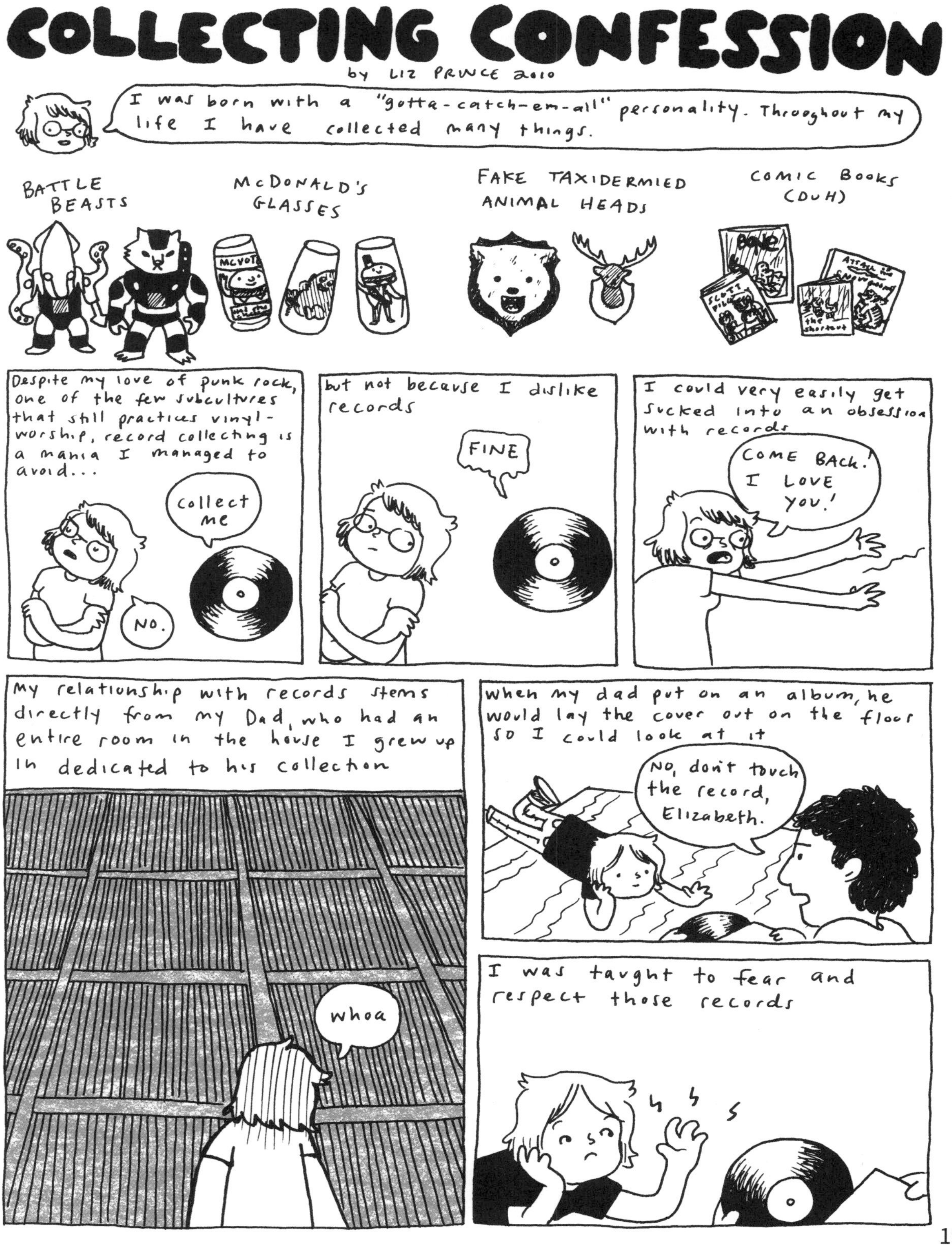
COLLECTING CONFESSION
by LIZ PRINCE 2010
I was born with a "gotta-catch-em-all" personality. Throughout my life I have collected many things.
BATTLE BEASTS
McDONALD'S GLASSES
FAKE TAXIDERMIED ANIMAL HEADS
COMIC BOOKS (DUH)
Despite my love of punk rock, one of the few subcultures that still practices vinyl-worship, record collecting is a mania I managed to avoid...
collect me
NO.
but not because I dislike records
FINE
I could very easily get sucked into an obsession with records
COME BACK! I LOVE YOU!
My relationship with records stems directly from my Dad, who had an entire room in the house I grew up in dedicated to his collection
whoa
when my dad put on an album, he would lay the cover out on the floor so I could look at it
No, don't touch the record, Elizabeth.
I was taught to fear and respect those records

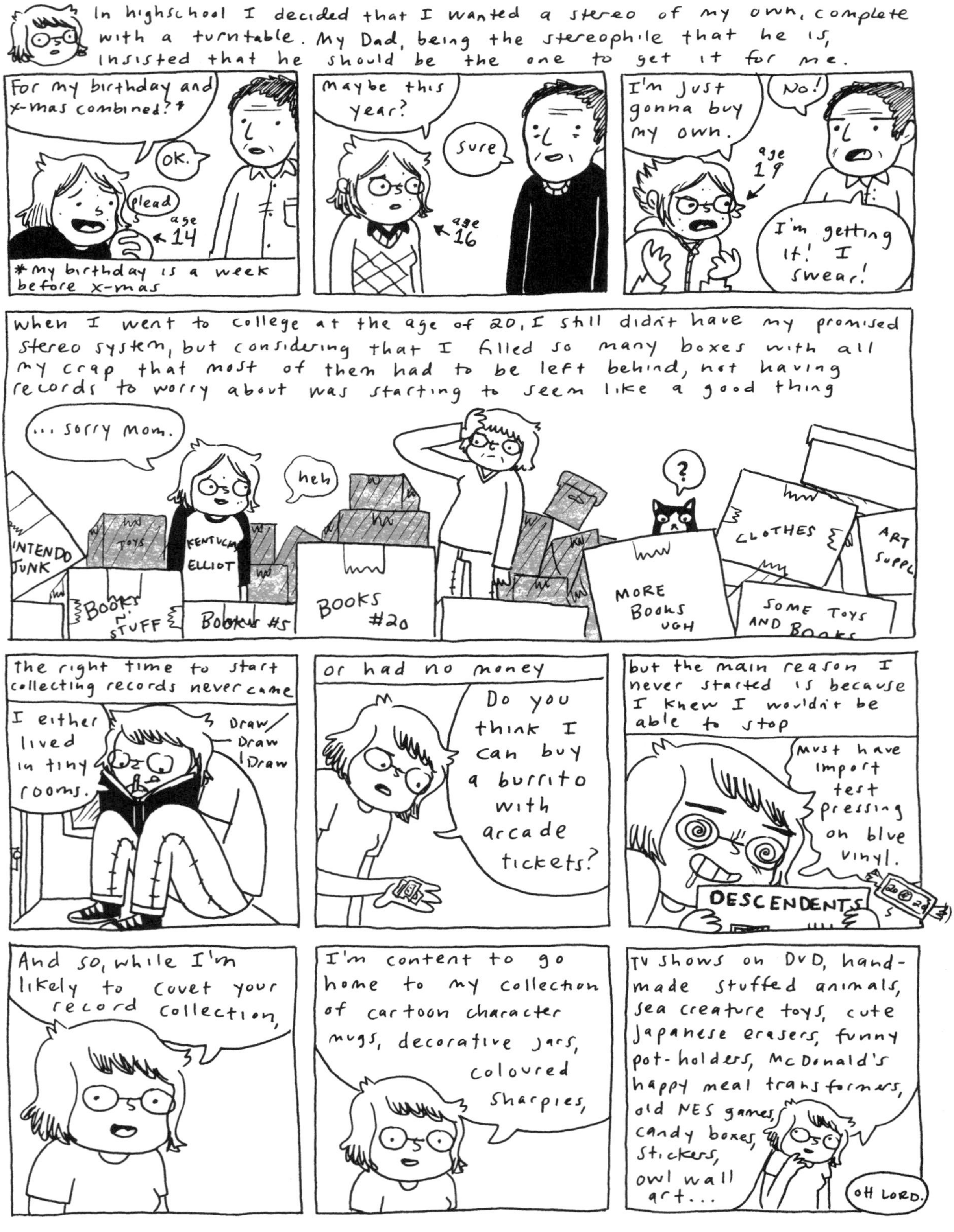
In highschool I decided that I wanted a stereo of my own, complete with a turntable. My Dad, being the stereophile that he is, insisted that he should be the one to get it for me.
For my birthday and x-mas combined?*
OK.
plead
age 14
*my birthday is a week before x-mas
Maybe this year?
sure
age 16
I'm just gonna buy my own.
No!
age 19
I'm getting it! I swear!
when I went to college at the age of 20, I still didn't have my promised stereo system, but considering that I filled so many boxes with all my crap that most of them had to be left behind, not having records to worry about was starting to seem like a good thing
... sorry mom.
heh
?
TOYS
KENTUCKY
ELLIOT
INTENDO JUNK
BOOKS N' STUFF
Books #5
BOOKS #20
MORE BOOKS UGH
CLOTHES
ART SUPPL
SOME TOYS AND BOOKS
the right time to start collecting records never came
I either lived in tiny rooms.
Draw/ Draw/ Draw
or had no money
Do you think I can buy a burrito with arcade tickets?
but the main reason I never started is because I knew I wouldn't be able to stop
Must have import test pressing on blue vinyl.
DESCENDENTS
And so, while I'm likely to covet your record collection,
I'm content to go home to my collection of cartoon character mugs, decorative jars, coloured sharpies,
TV shows on DVD, hand-made stuffed animals, sea creature toys, cute Japanese erasers, funny pot-holders, McDonald's happy meal transformers, old NES games, candy boxes, stickers, owl wall art...
OH LORD.

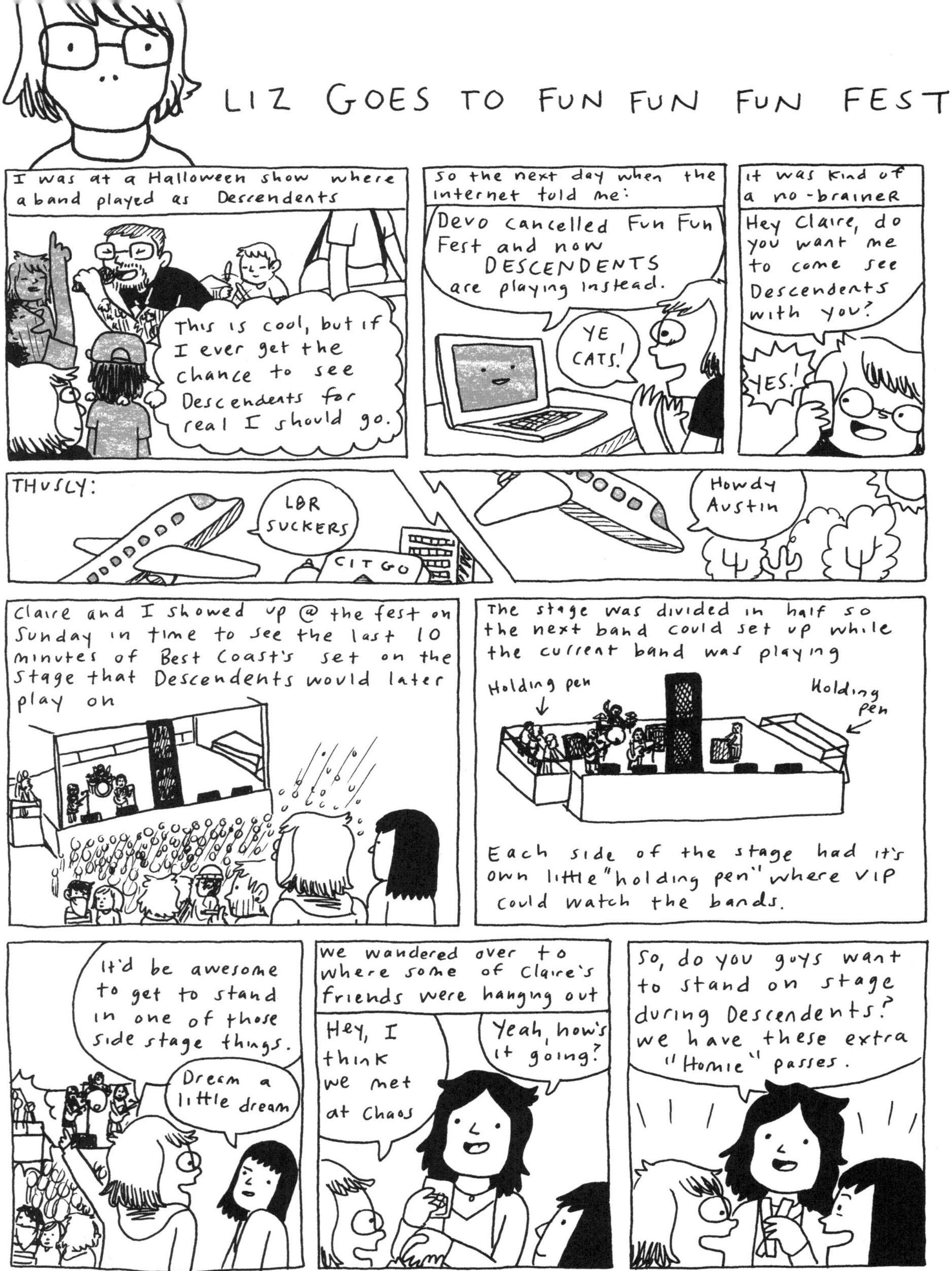

LIZ GOES TO FUN FUN FUN FEST
I was at a Halloween show where a band played as Descendents
This is cool, but if I ever get the chance to see Descendents for real I should go.
so the next day when the internet told me:
Devo cancelled Fun Fun Fest and now DESCENDENTS are playing instead.
YE CATS!
it was kind of a no-brainer
Hey Claire, do you want me to come see Descendents with you?
YES!
THUSLY:
LBR SUCKERS
CITGO
Howdy Austin
Claire and I showed up @ the fest on Sunday in time to see the last 10 minutes of Best Coast's set on the stage that Descendents would later play on
The stage was divided in half so the next band could set up while the current band was playing
Holding pen
Holding pen
Each side of the stage had it's own little "holding pen" where VIP could watch the bands.
It'd be awesome to get to stand in one of those side stage things.
Dream a little dream
we wandered over to where some of Claire's friends were hanging out
Hey, I think we met at Chaos
Yeah, how's it going?
So, do you guys want to stand on stage during Descendents? we have these extra "Homie" passes.

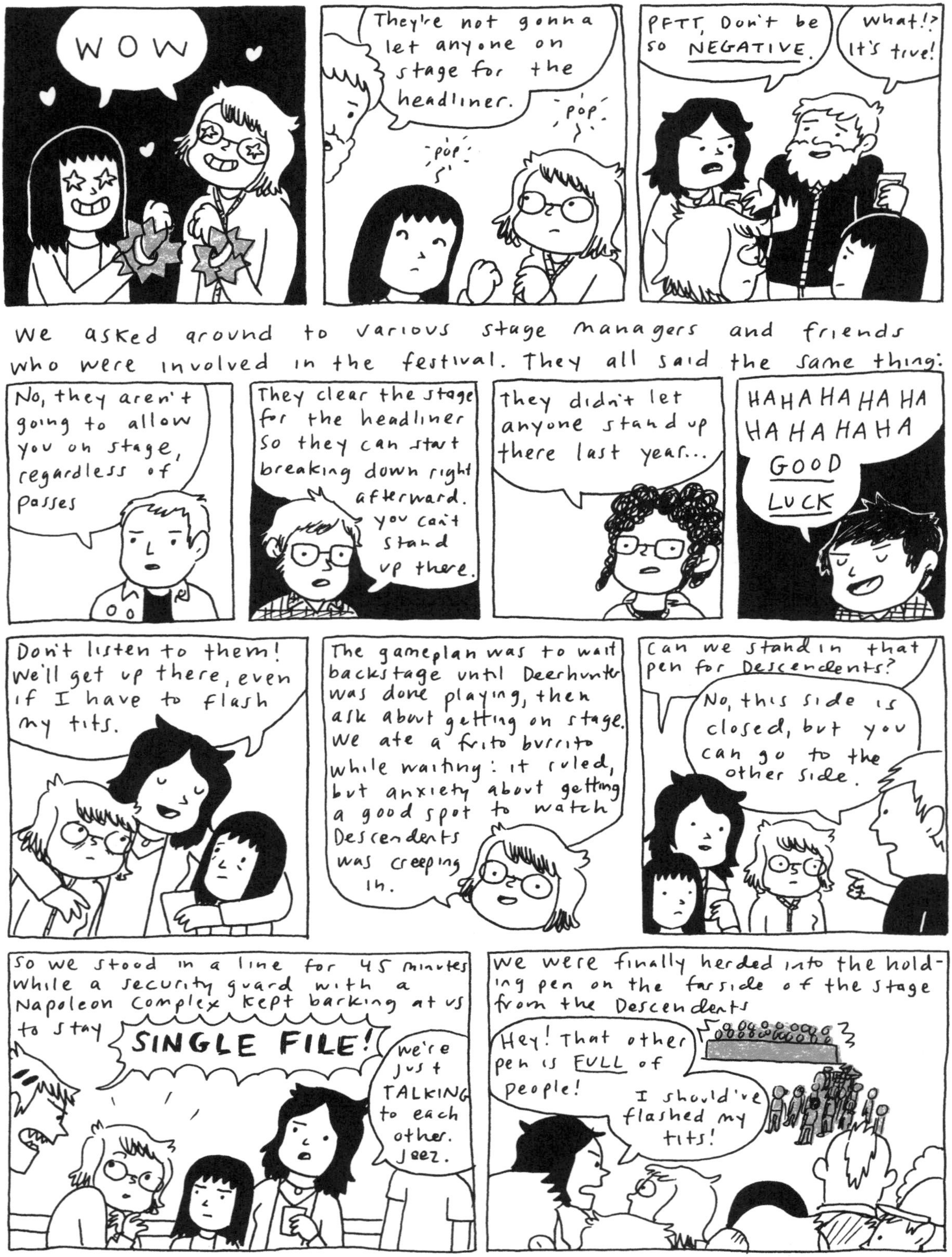
WOW
They're not gonna let anyone on stage for the headliner.
POP
POP
PFTT, Don't be so NEGATIVE.
What!? It's true!
We asked around to various stage managers and friends who were involved in the festival. They all said the same thing:
No, they aren't going to allow you on stage, regardless of passes
They clear the stage for the headliner so they can start breaking down right afterward. You can't stand up there.
They didn't let anyone stand up there last year...
HAHAHAHAHA HAHAHAHA GOOD LUCK
Don't listen to them! We'll get up there, even if I have to flash my tits.
The gameplan was to wait backstage until Deerhunter was done playing, then ask about getting on stage. We ate a frito burrito while waiting: it ruled, but anxiety about getting a good spot to watch Descendents was creeping in.
Can we stand in that pen for Descendents?
No, this side is closed, but you can go to the other side.
So we stood in a line for 45 minutes while a security guard with a Napoleon Complex kept barking at us to stay
SINGLE FILE!
We're just TALKING to each other. Jeez.
We were finally herded into the holding pen on the farside of the stage from the Descendents
Hey! That other pen is FULL of people!
I should've flashed my tits!

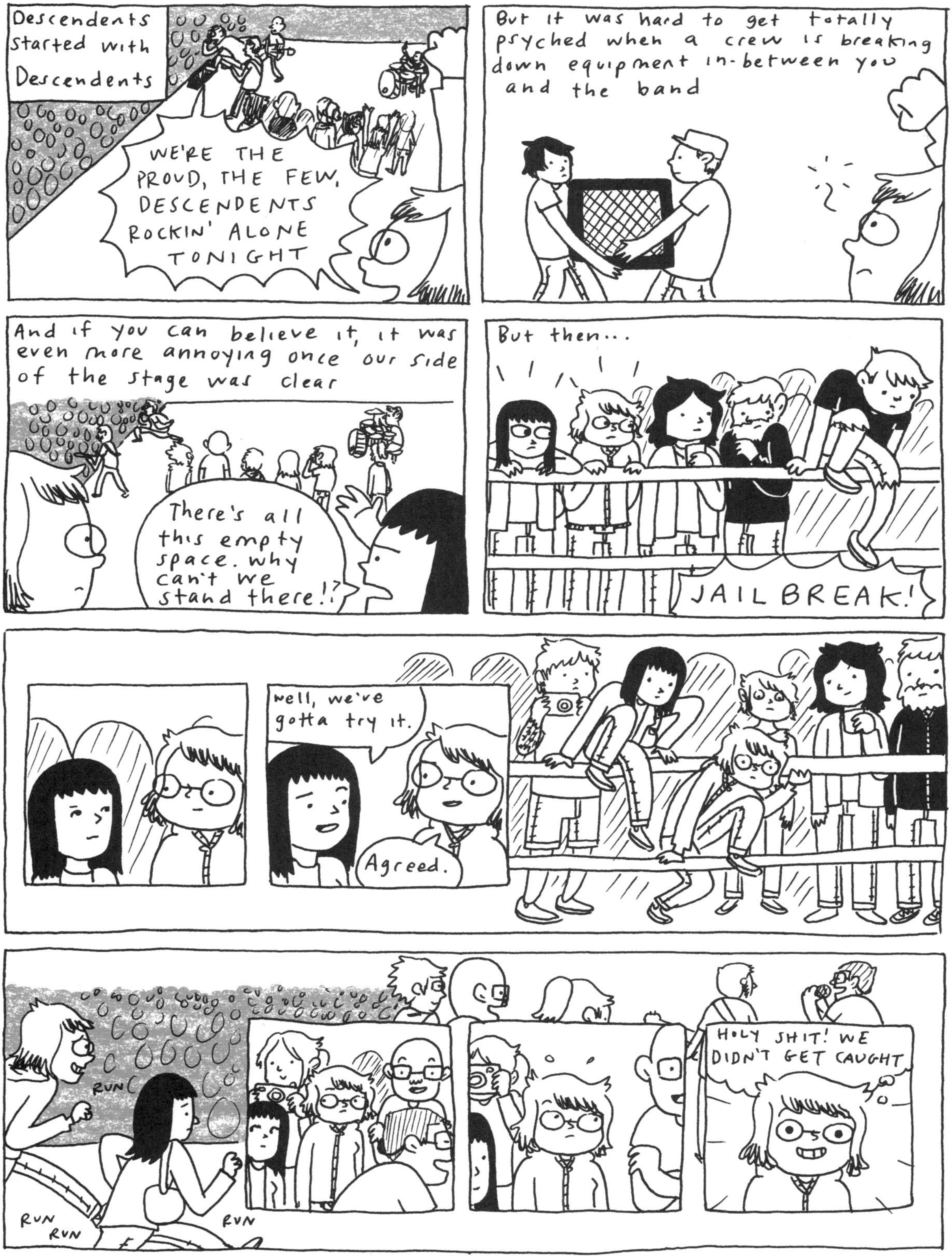
Descendents started with Descendents
WE'RE THE PROUD, THE FEW, DESCENDENTS ROCKIN' ALONE TONIGHT
But it was hard to get totally psyched when a crew is breaking down equipment in-between you and the band
And if you can believe it, it was even more annoying once our side of the stage was clear
There's all this empty space. why can't we stand there!?
But then...
JAIL BREAK!
well, we've gotta try it.
Agreed.
RUN
RUN RUN
RUN
HOLY SHIT! WE DIDN'T GET CAUGHT

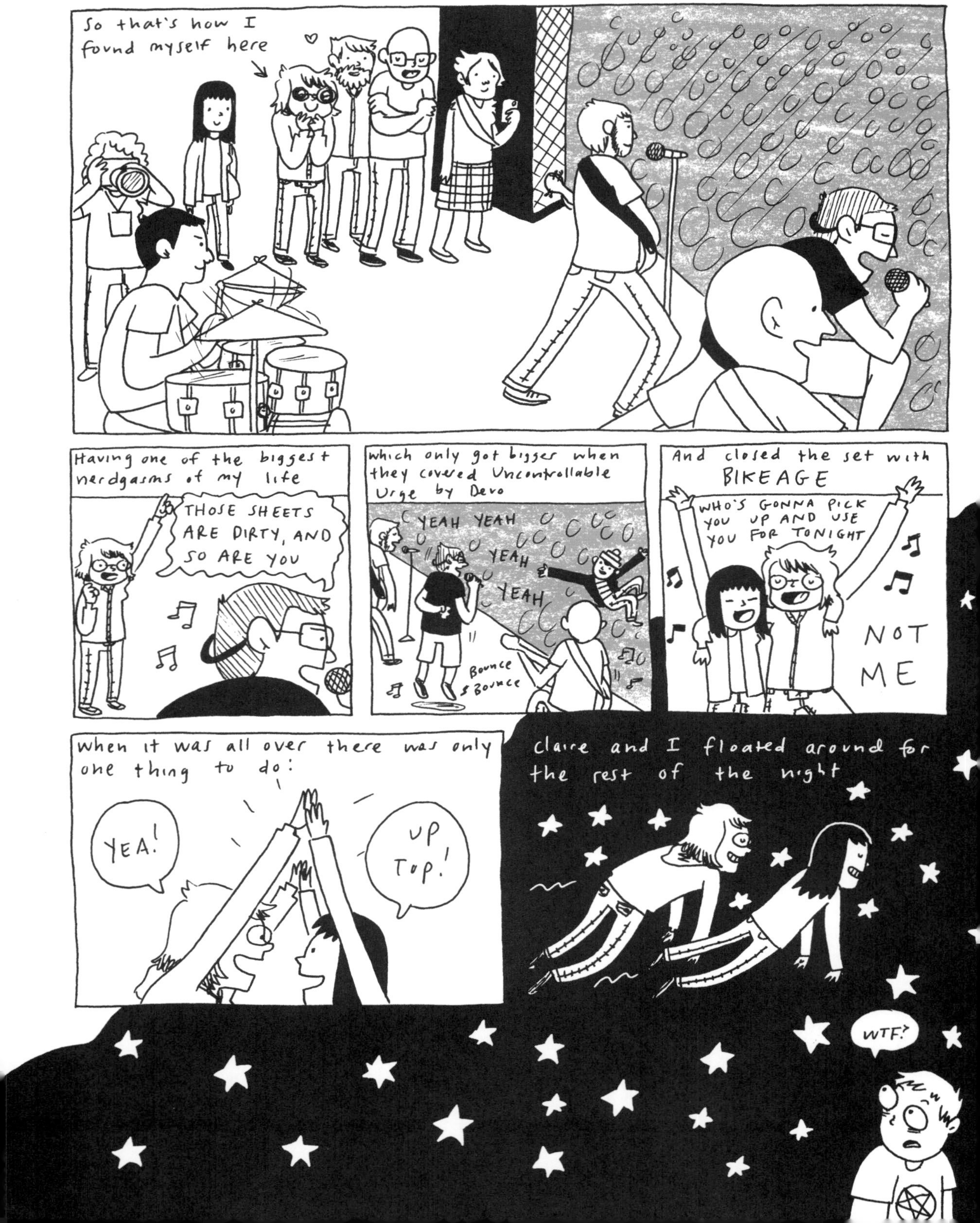
So that's how I found myself here
Having one of the biggest nerdgasms of my life
THOSE SHEETS ARE DIRTY, AND SO ARE YOU
which only got bigger when they covered Uncontrollable Urge by Devo
YEAH YEAH
YEAH
YEAH
Bounce
Bounce
And closed the set with BIKEAGE
WHO'S GONNA PICK YOU UP AND USE YOU FOR TONIGHT
NOT ME
When it was all over there was only one thing to do:
YEA!
UP TOP!
Claire and I floated around for the rest of the night
WTF?

Hell, I'll probably float around on that high for the rest of my life
Daddy, why does Grandma float around like that?
who wants COOKIES?
Try to ignore it.
And that's what I'll be like when I get old.
... sorry.

OOPS! When I originally drew this comic, it was for the internet, so I didn't have to pay attention to page length. Lucky for you, I have some extra junk related to this comic to fill the empty space!

89323
HOMIE PASS
FÜNF
UNF
UNfest

The "Homie Pass" is an all-access backstage pass that denotes you are a friend of one the bands performing at the fest.

DESCEND
COOLIDGE
BEAR
ROTTING
NOTHING WOU YOU
MUG
HOPE
SOUR
POP
SHE DON'T CARE
MY AGE
I'M THE ONE
WHEN I GET OLD
TALKING
GROW UP
FOOD
CHEER
SUBURBAN
SILLY
EVERYTHING
CLEAN
PERVERT
GET THE TIME
WEINER
LOSER
ALL
Uncontrol
Bike

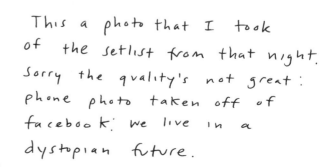

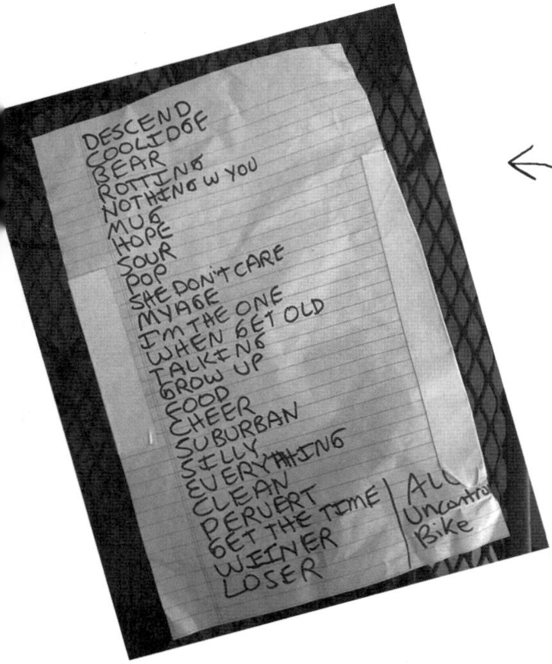

This a photo that I took of the setlist from that night. Sorry the quality's not great: phone photo taken off of facebook: we live in a dystopian future.

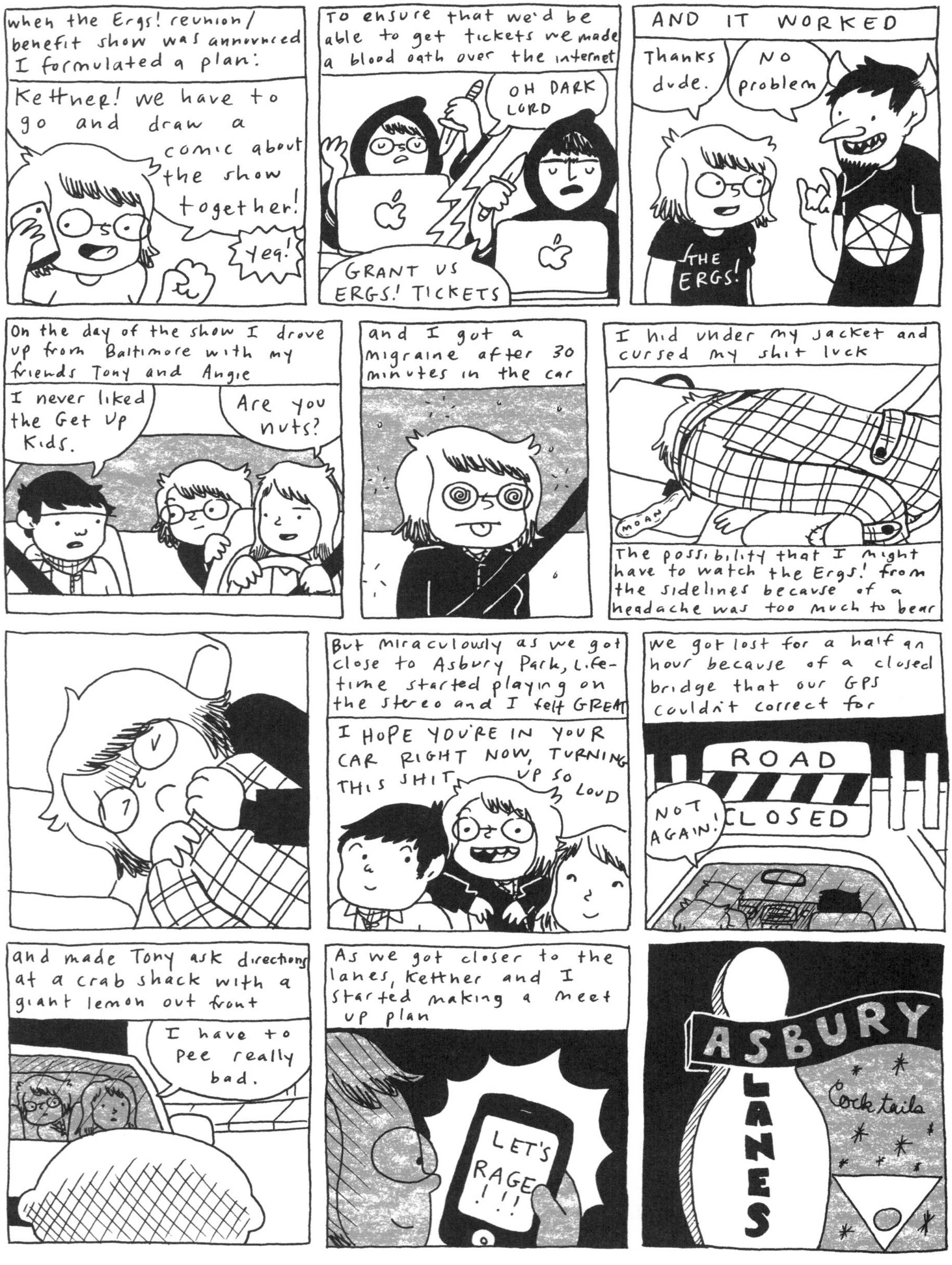
when the Ergs! reunion/ benefit show was announced I formulated a plan:
Kettner! we have to go and draw a comic about the show together!
Yeq!
To ensure that we'd be able to get tickets we made a blood oath over the internet
OH DARK LORD
GRANT US ERGS! TICKETS
AND IT WORKED
Thanks dude.
NO problem
THE ERGS!
On the day of the show I drove up from Baltimore with my friends Tony and Angie
I never liked the Get Up Kids.
Are you nuts?
and I got a migraine after 30 minutes in the car
I hid under my jacket and cursed my shit luck
MOAN
The possibility that I might have to watch the Ergs! from the sidelines because of a headache was too much to bear
But miraculously as we got close to Asbury Park, Lifetime started playing on the stereo and I felt GREAT
I HOPE YOU'RE IN YOUR CAR RIGHT NOW, TURNING THIS SHIT UP SO LOUD
We got lost for a half an hour because of a closed bridge that our GPS couldn't correct for
ROAD CLOSED
NOT AGAIN!
and made Tony ask directions at a crab shack with a giant lemon out front
I have to pee really bad.
As we got closer to the lanes, Kettner and I started making a meet up plan
LET'S RAGE!!!
ASBURY LANES
Cocktails

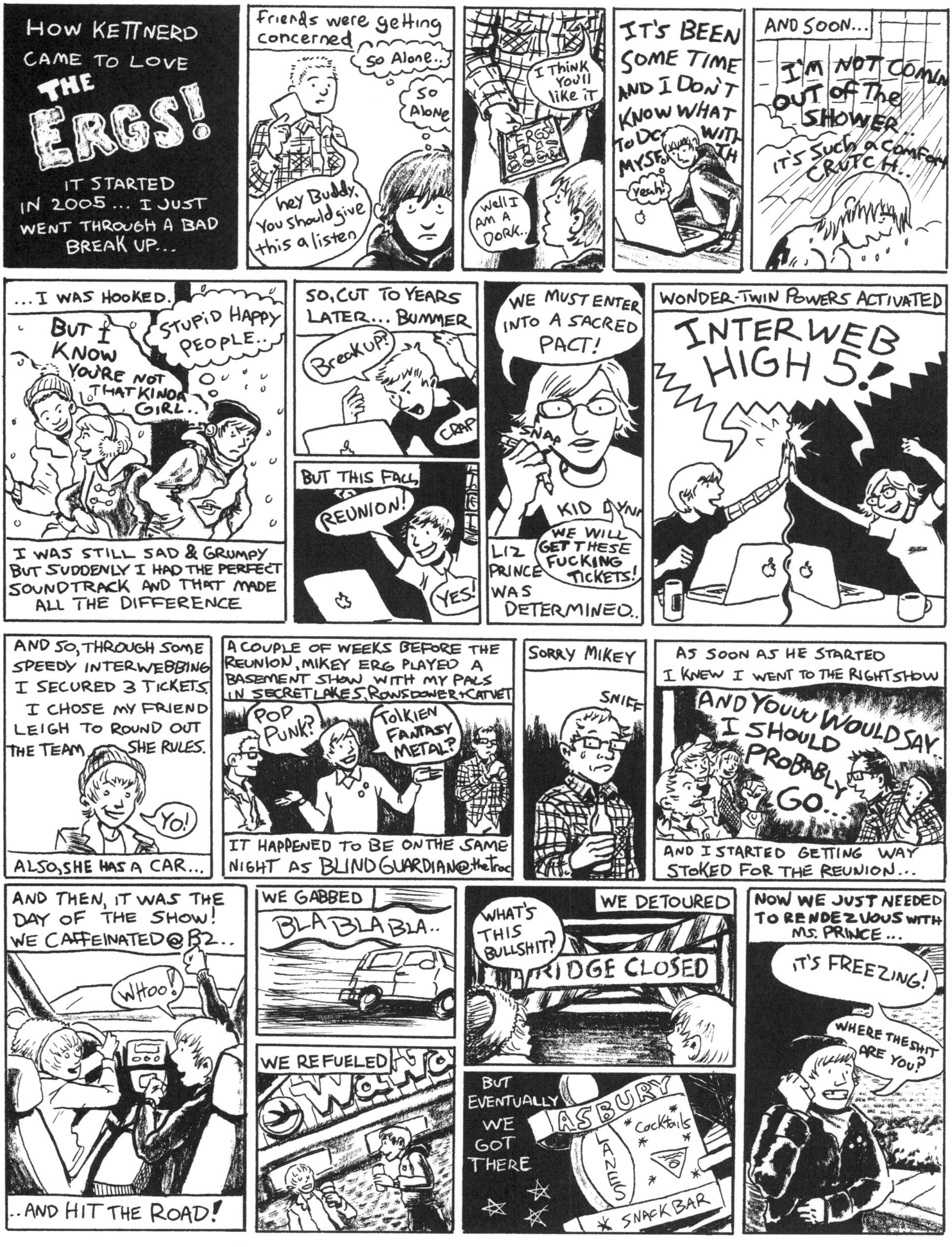
HOW KETTNERD CAME TO LOVE THE ERGS!
IT STARTED IN 2005... I JUST WENT THROUGH A BAD BREAK UP...
Friends were getting concerned
So Alone..
So Alone
hey Buddy, You should give this a listen
I Think You'll like it
well I AM A DORK..
IT'S BEEN SOME TIME AND I DON'T KNOW WHAT TO DO WITH MYSELF
Yeah!
AND SOON...
I'M NOT COMIN OUT OF THE SHOWER... IT'S SUCH A COMFORT CRUTCH..
...I WAS HOOKED.
BUT I KNOW YOU'RE NOT THAT KINDA GIRL..
STUPID HAPPY PEOPLE..
I WAS STILL SAD & GRUMPY BUT SUDDENLY I HAD THE PERFECT SOUNDTRACK AND THAT MADE ALL THE DIFFERENCE
SO, CUT TO YEARS LATER... BUMMER
BreakUP?
CRAP
BUT THIS FALL,
REUNION!
YES!
WE MUST ENTER INTO A SACRED PACT!
SNAP
KID DYN
WE WILL GET THESE FUCKING TICKETS!
LIZ PRINCE WAS DETERMINED..
WONDER-TWIN POWERS ACTIVATED
INTERWEB HIGH 5!
AND SO, THROUGH SOME SPEEDY INTERWEBBING I SECURED 3 TICKETS. I CHOSE MY FRIEND LEIGH TO ROUND OUT THE TEAM. SHE RULES.
Yo!
ALSO, SHE HAS A CAR...
A COUPLE OF WEEKS BEFORE THE REUNION, MIKEY ERG PLAYED A BASEMENT SHOW WITH MY PALS IN SECRET LAKES, ROWSDOWER + CATVET
POP PUNK?
TOLKIEN FANTASY METAL?
IT HAPPENED TO BE ON THE SAME NIGHT AS BLIND GUARDIAN @ the Troc
SORRY MIKEY
SNIFF
AS SOON AS HE STARTED I KNEW I WENT TO THE RIGHT SHOW
AND YOUUU WOULD SAY I SHOULD PROBABLY GO...
AND I STARTED GETTING WAY STOKED FOR THE REUNION...
AND THEN, IT WAS THE DAY OF THE SHOW! WE CAFFEINATED @ B2...
WHOO!
..AND HIT THE ROAD!
WE GABBED
BLA BLA BLA..
WE REFUELED
WE DETOURED
WHAT'S THIS BULLSHIT?
RIDGE CLOSED
BUT EVENTUALLY WE GOT THERE
ASBURY LANES
Cocktails
SNACK BAR
NOW WE JUST NEEDED TO RENDEZVOUS WITH MS. PRINCE...
IT'S FREEZING!
WHERE THE SHIT ARE YOU?

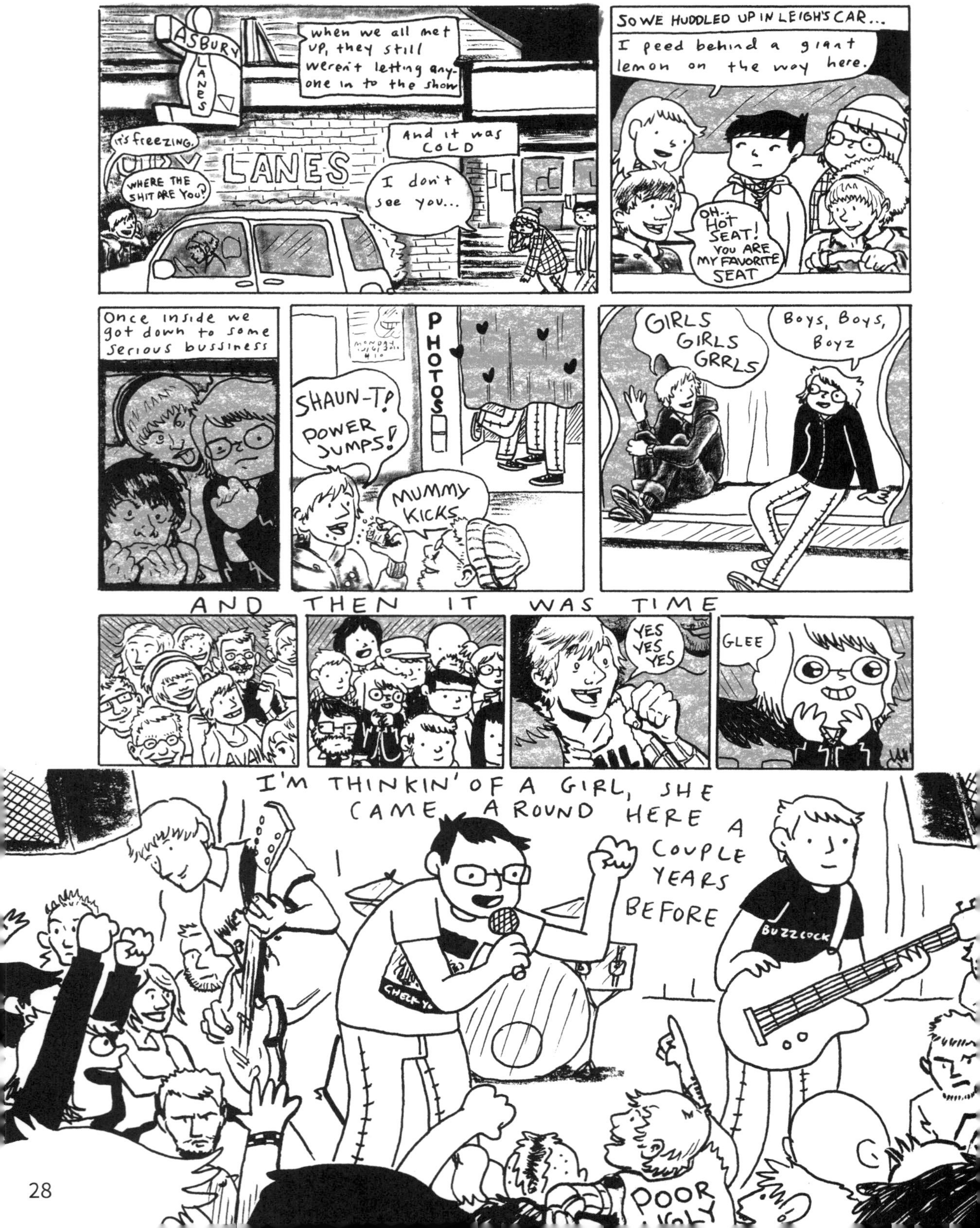

when we all met up, they still weren't letting anyone in to the show
ASBURY LANES
it's freezing.
WHERE THE SHIT ARE YOU?
LANES
And it was COLD
I don't see you...
SO WE HUDDLED UP IN LEIGH'S CAR...
I peed behind a giant lemon on the way here.
OH.. HOT SEAT! YOU ARE MY FAVORITE SEAT
Once inside we got down to some serious bussiness
PHOTOS
SHAUN-T! POWER JUMPS!
MUMMY KICKS
GIRLS GIRLS GRRLS
Boys, Boys, Boyz
AND THEN IT WAS TIME
YES YES YES
GLEE
I'M THINKIN' OF A GIRL, SHE CAME AROUND HERE A COUPLE YEARS BEFORE
BUZZCOCK
POOR

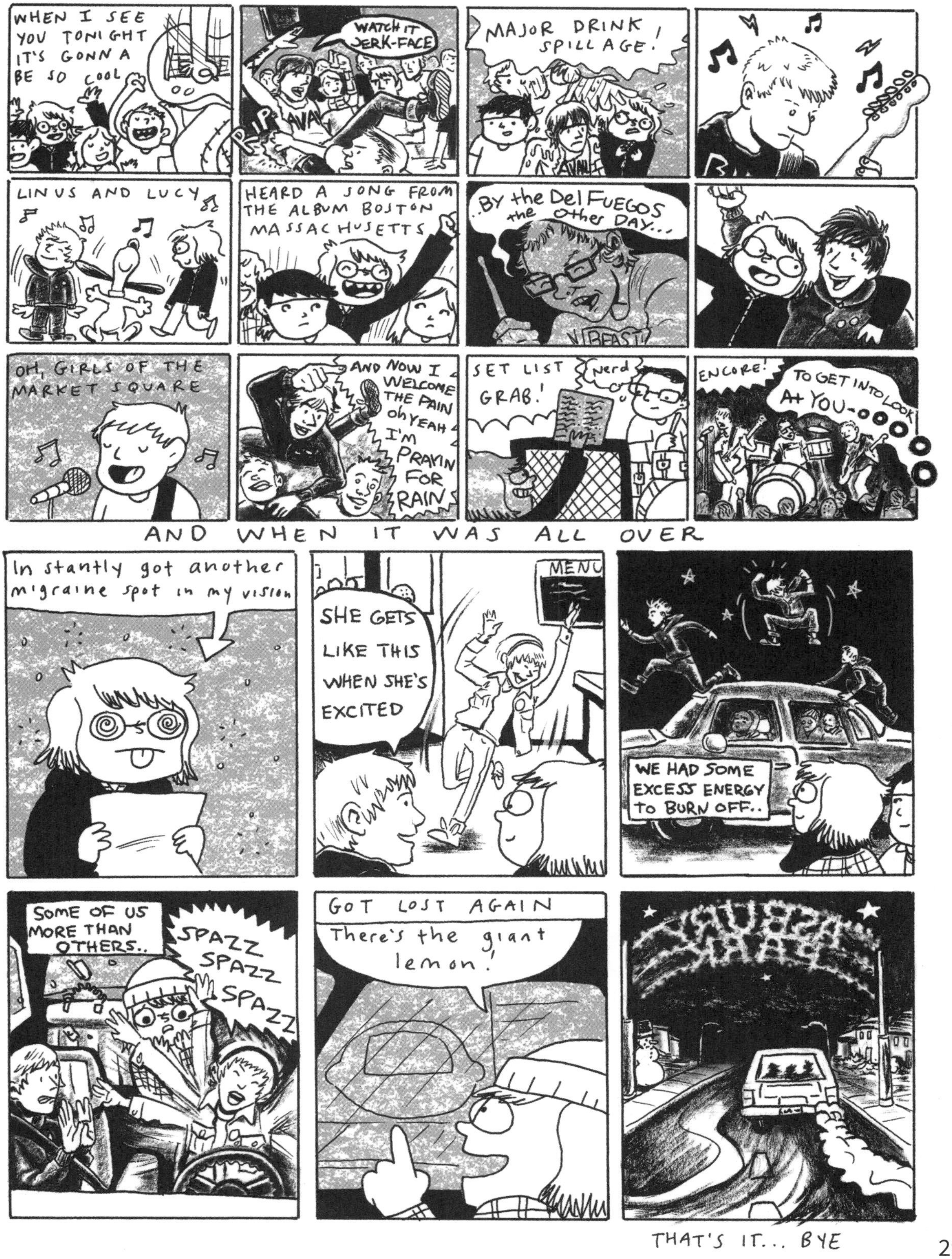
WHEN I SEE YOU TONIGHT IT'S GONNA BE SO COOL
WATCH IT JERK-FACE
RIP
MAJOR DRINK SPILLAGE!
LINUS AND LUCY
HEARD A SONG FROM THE ALBUM BOSTON MASSACHUSETTS
..BY the Del Fuegos the other DAY...
OH, GIRLS OF THE MARKET SQUARE
AND NOW I WELCOME THE PAIN oh YEAH I'M PRAYIN FOR RAIN
SET LIST GRAB!
Nerd
ENCORE!
TO GET INTO LOOK AT YOU-OOOO
AND WHEN IT WAS ALL OVER
In stantly got another migraine spot in my vision
MENU
SHE GETS LIKE THIS WHEN SHE'S EXCITED
WE HAD SOME EXCESS ENERGY TO BURN OFF..
SOME OF US MORE THAN OTHERS..
SPAZZ SPAZZ SPAZZ
GOT LOST AGAIN
There's the giant lemon!
THAT'S IT... BYE

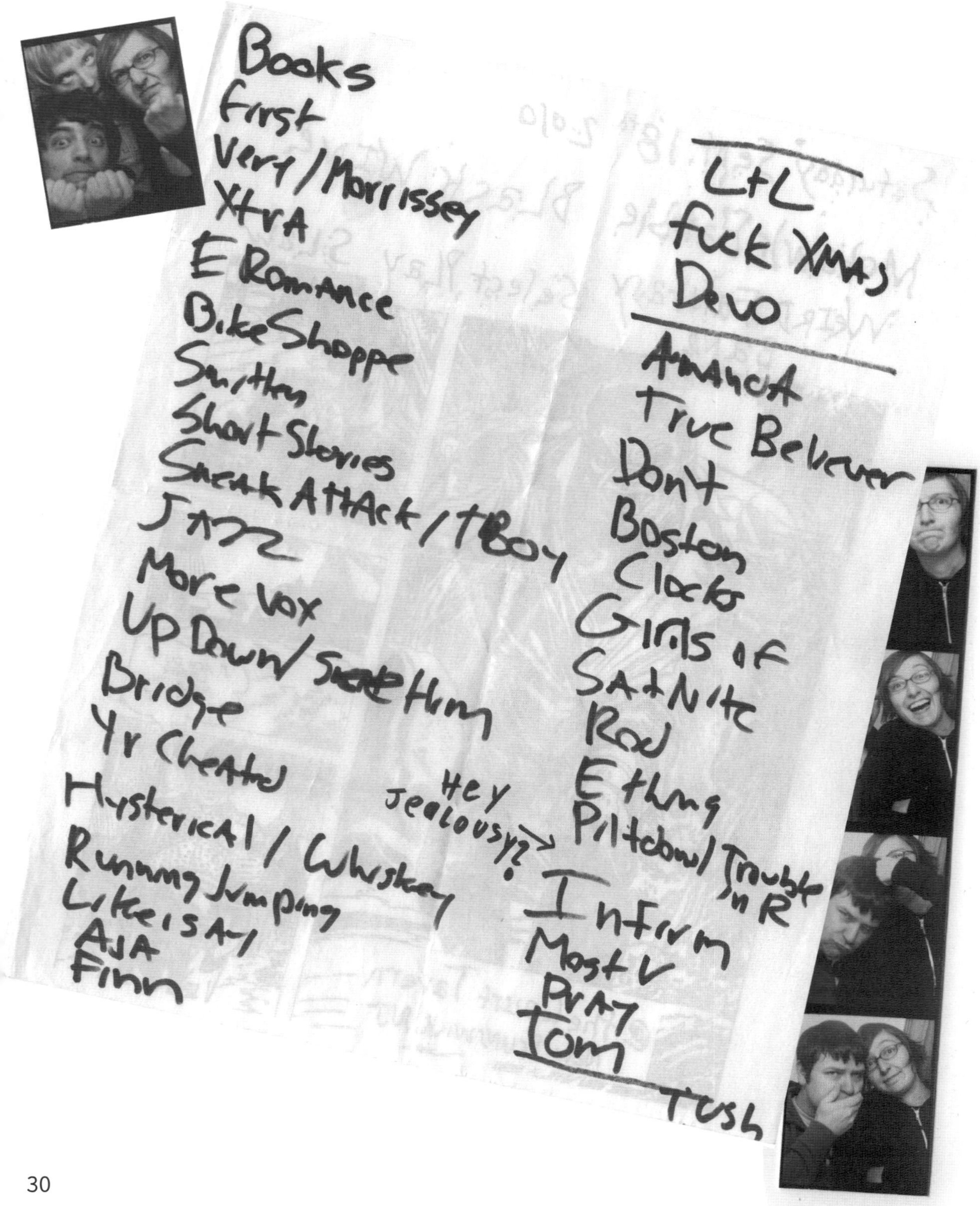

Books
First
Very / Morrissey
Xtra
E Romance
Bike Shoppe
Smitten
Short Stories
Sneak Attack / T Boy
Jazz
More Vox
Up Down / Sneak Him
Bridge
Yr Cheated
Hysterical / Whiskey
Running Jumping
Like i Say
Aja
Finn

Hey Jealousy? →

LtL
Fuck Xmas
Devo

Amanda
True Believer
Don't
Boston
Clocks
Girls of Sat Nite
Rod
E thing
Piltdown / Trouble in R
I Inform
Most V
Pray
Tom

Tush

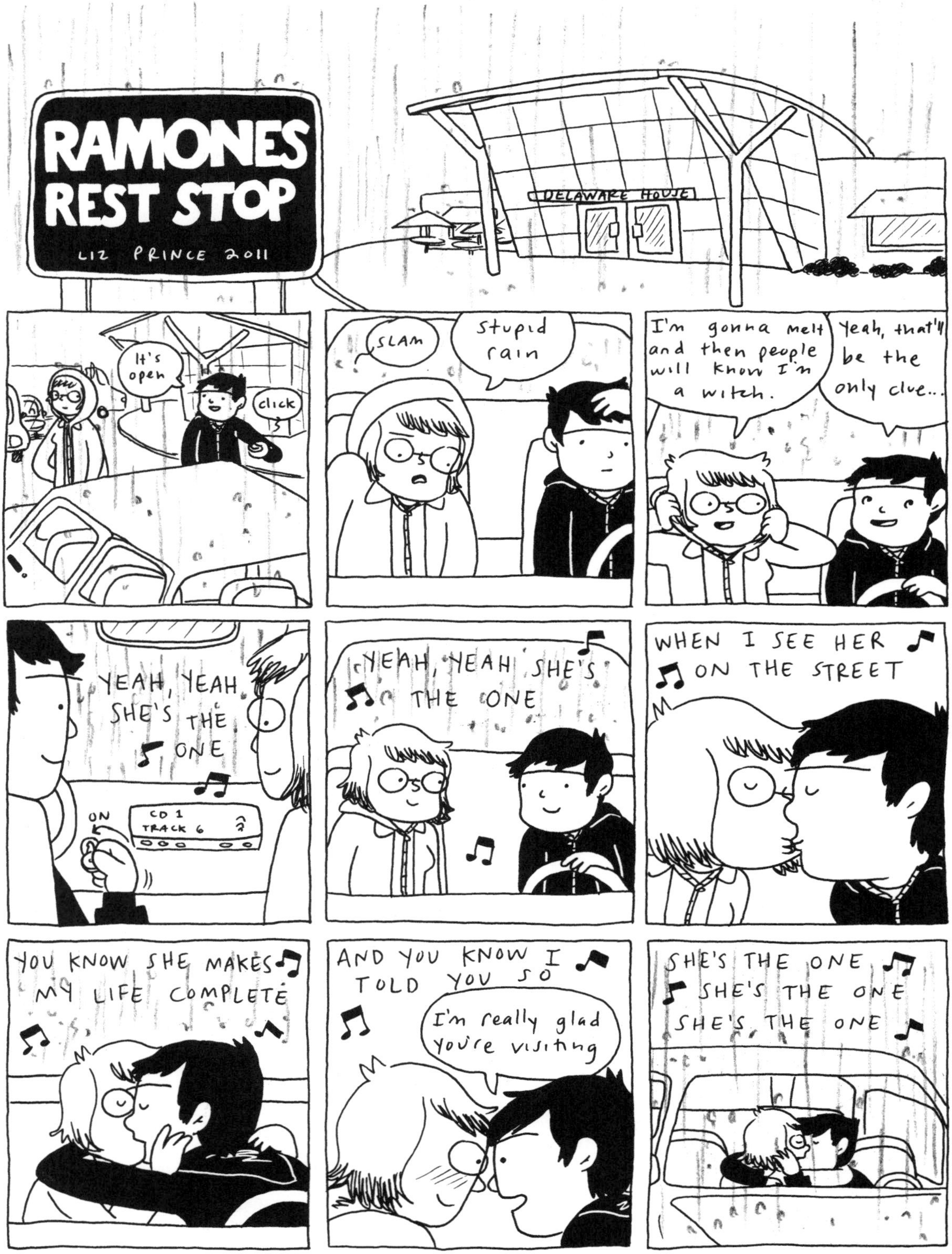
RAMONES REST STOP
LIZ PRINCE 2011
DELAWARE HOUSE
It's open
click
SLAM
Stupid rain
I'm gonna melt and then people will know I'm a witch.
Yeah, that'll be the only clue...
YEAH, YEAH SHE'S THE ONE
ON
CD 1 TRACK 6
YEAH, YEAH SHE'S THE ONE
WHEN I SEE HER ON THE STREET
YOU KNOW SHE MAKES MY LIFE COMPLETE
AND YOU KNOW I TOLD YOU SO
I'm really glad you're visiting
SHE'S THE ONE
SHE'S THE ONE
SHE'S THE ONE

MY standard break from life

LIZ PRINCE 2011

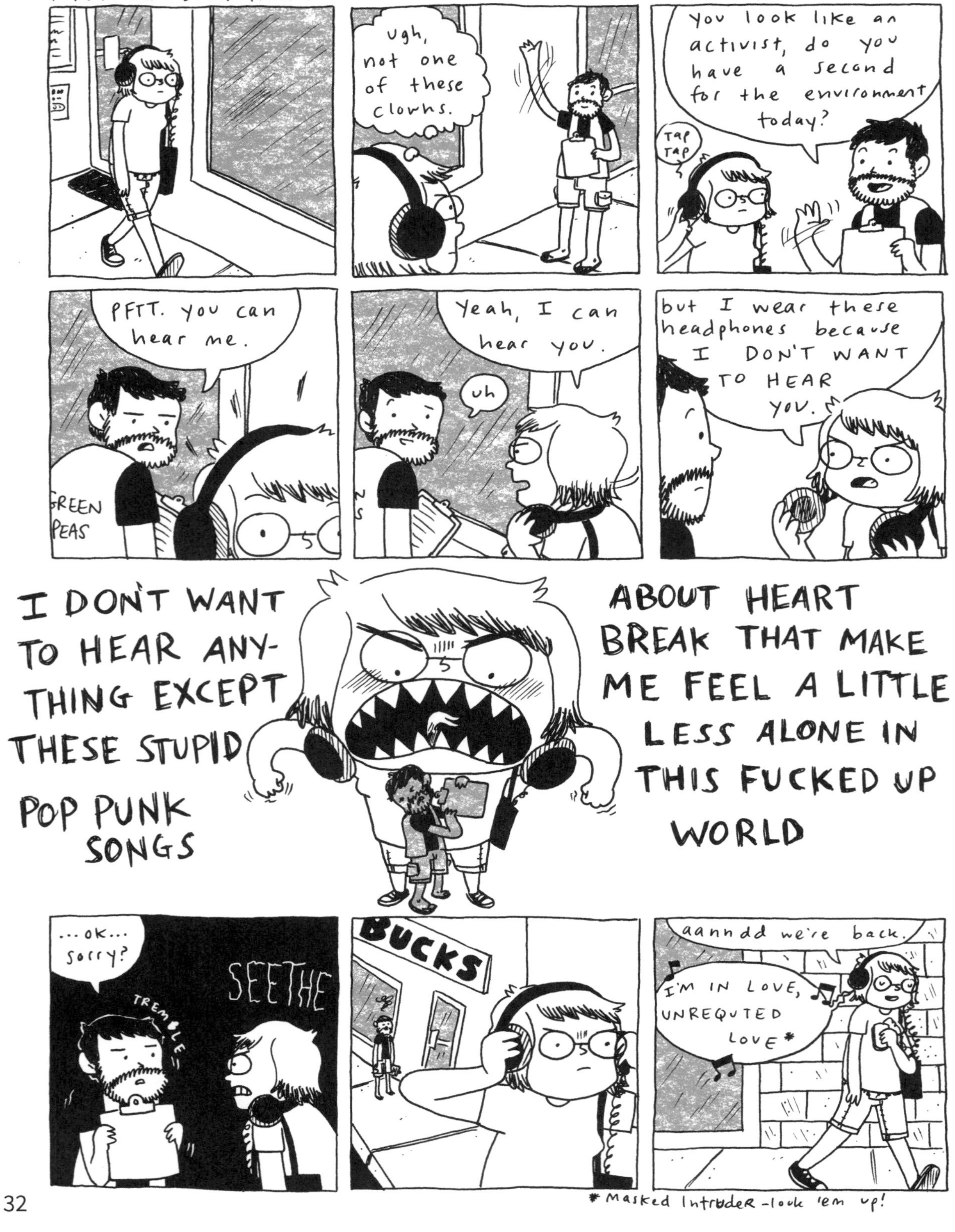
ugh, not one of these clowns.
You look like an activist, do you have a second for the environment today?
TAP TAP
PFTT. you can hear me.
GREEN PEAS
Yeah, I can hear you.
uh
but I wear these headphones because I DON'T WANT TO HEAR YOU.
I DON'T WANT TO HEAR ANY-THING EXCEPT THESE STUPID POP PUNK SONGS
ABOUT HEART BREAK THAT MAKE ME FEEL A LITTLE LESS ALONE IN THIS FUCKED UP WORLD
...ok... sorry?
TREMBLE
SEETHE
BUCKS
aannd we're back.
I'M IN LOVE, UNREQUTED LOVE*

* Masked Intruder - look 'em up!

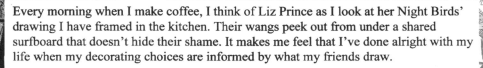

Hello, my name is Todd Taylor.

Every morning when I make coffee, I think of Liz Prince as I look at her Night Birds' drawing I have framed in the kitchen. Their wangs peek out from under a shared surfboard that doesn't hide their shame. It makes me feel that I've done alright with my life when my decorating choices are informed by what my friends draw.

I'm the founder/editor for Razorcake, a bi-monthly fanzine since 2001. We're the only official 501(c)(3) non-profit music magazine in America. Razorcake specializes in non-asshole weirdos who have a deep love and appreciation of DIY punk, because that's who we are. We acknowledge the culture's deep past and celebrate the almost-hidden strands of amazing punk that are currently being created. Our volunteer staff is made up of marginalized gender, ethnic, and class voices—in an often misunderstood, misrepresented form of music.

I don't think I've told Liz this. She first got on my radar because she drew an awesome comic where she was dreaming she was in a band and that band was featured on the cover of *Razorcake*. It was incredibly flattering. DIY punk, if you're in it for more than a couple of years, is two or three degrees of separation. We both grew up in small desert towns. We knew several of the same people. When we finally met face-to-face at adjacent tables at LA Zine Fest, we shared undeniably overlapping Venn diagrams of common ground.

Yes, now would be an awesome time for me to remember how Liz started contributing to *Razorcake*, but my best guess is that either she asked me or I asked her. Nothing fancy. My usual pep talk to new contributors is this: Get. Your. Shit. Done. Well. And. On. Time. Liz didn't need the talk. Her talent is matched by her self-discipline and hustle. The end result has been a constant, uncomplicated collaboration and mutual appreciation for years. Our relationship would make awful reality TV.

"How you doing Liz?"
"Good. You, Todd?"
"Good. Rad comic. Thanks."
Publish, repeat.

Liz Prince isn't pretending in these pages collected from her *Razorcake* columns. She's not yearning to be something she's not. She's living. She's truthful and funny and sad and insightful and self-aware. She has a real knack for presenting penetrating social commentary in an almost casual way. She also has two cats, Wolfman and Dracula. Strap some webcams on those two because their antics would make great reality TV.

Liz's art is deceptively simple.
And simple isn't easy; neither is life.

Thanks, Liz.

RAZORCAKE
non-profit punk rock
#86
WE DO OUR PART
MARS DIXON
SHANNON THOMPSON

NON-PROFIT PUNK
ZORCAKE
#89

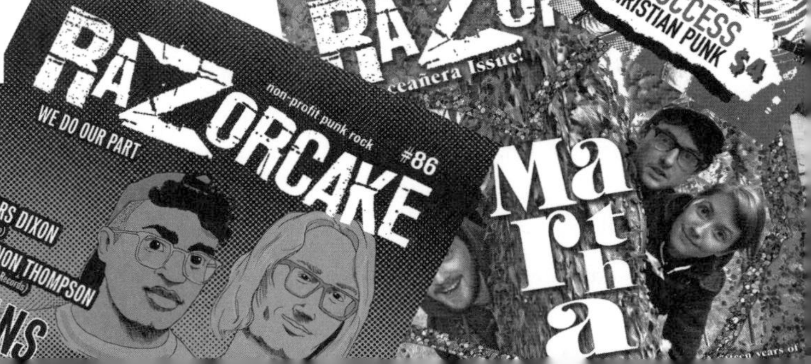

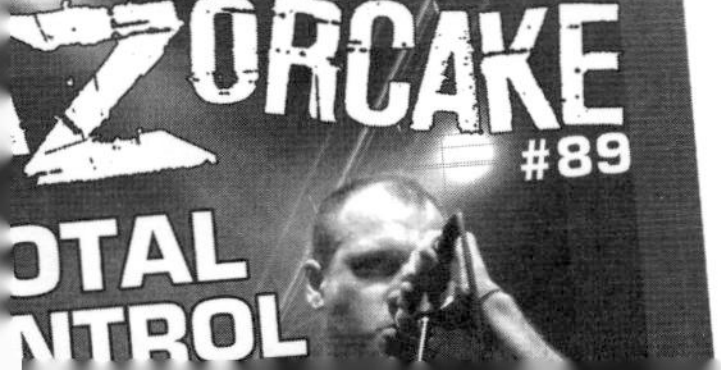

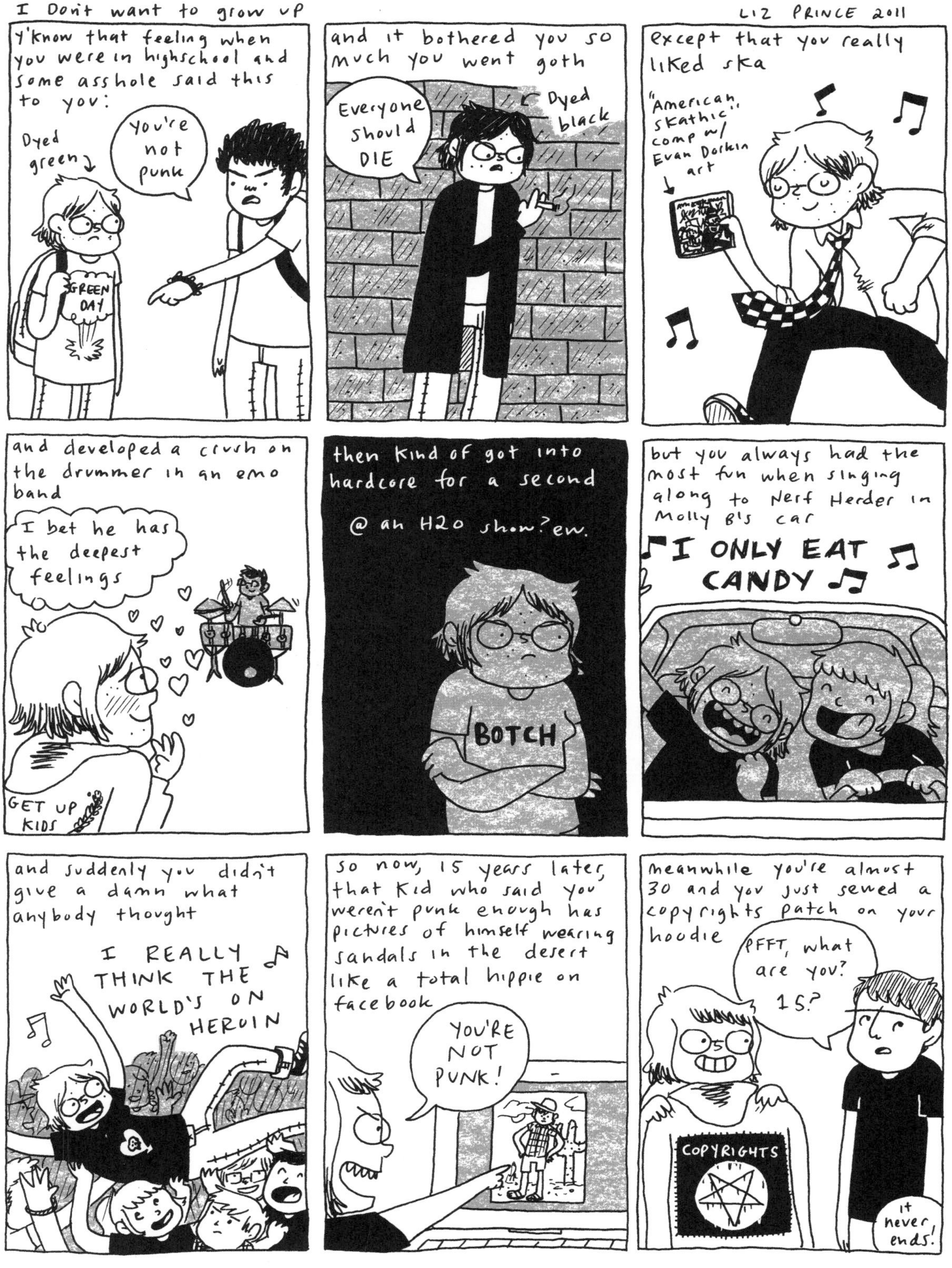
I Don't want to grow up
LIZ PRINCE 2011
Y'know that feeling when you were in highschool and some asshole said this to you:
Dyed green
You're not punk
GREEN DAY
and it bothered you so much you went goth
Everyone should DIE
Dyed black
except that you really liked ska
"American Skathic" comp w/ Evan Dorkin art
and developed a crush on the drummer in an emo band
I bet he has the deepest feelings
GET UP KIDS
then kind of got into hardcore for a second
@ an H2O show? ew.
BOTCH
but you always had the most fun when singing along to Nerf Herder in Molly B's car
I ONLY EAT CANDY
and suddenly you didn't give a damn what anybody thought
I REALLY THINK THE WORLD'S ON HEROIN
so now, 15 years later, that kid who said you weren't punk enough has pictures of himself wearing sandals in the desert like a total hippie on facebook
YOU'RE NOT PUNK!
meanwhile you're almost 30 and you just sewed a copyrights patch on your hoodie
PFFT, what are you? 15?
COPYRIGHTS
it never ends!

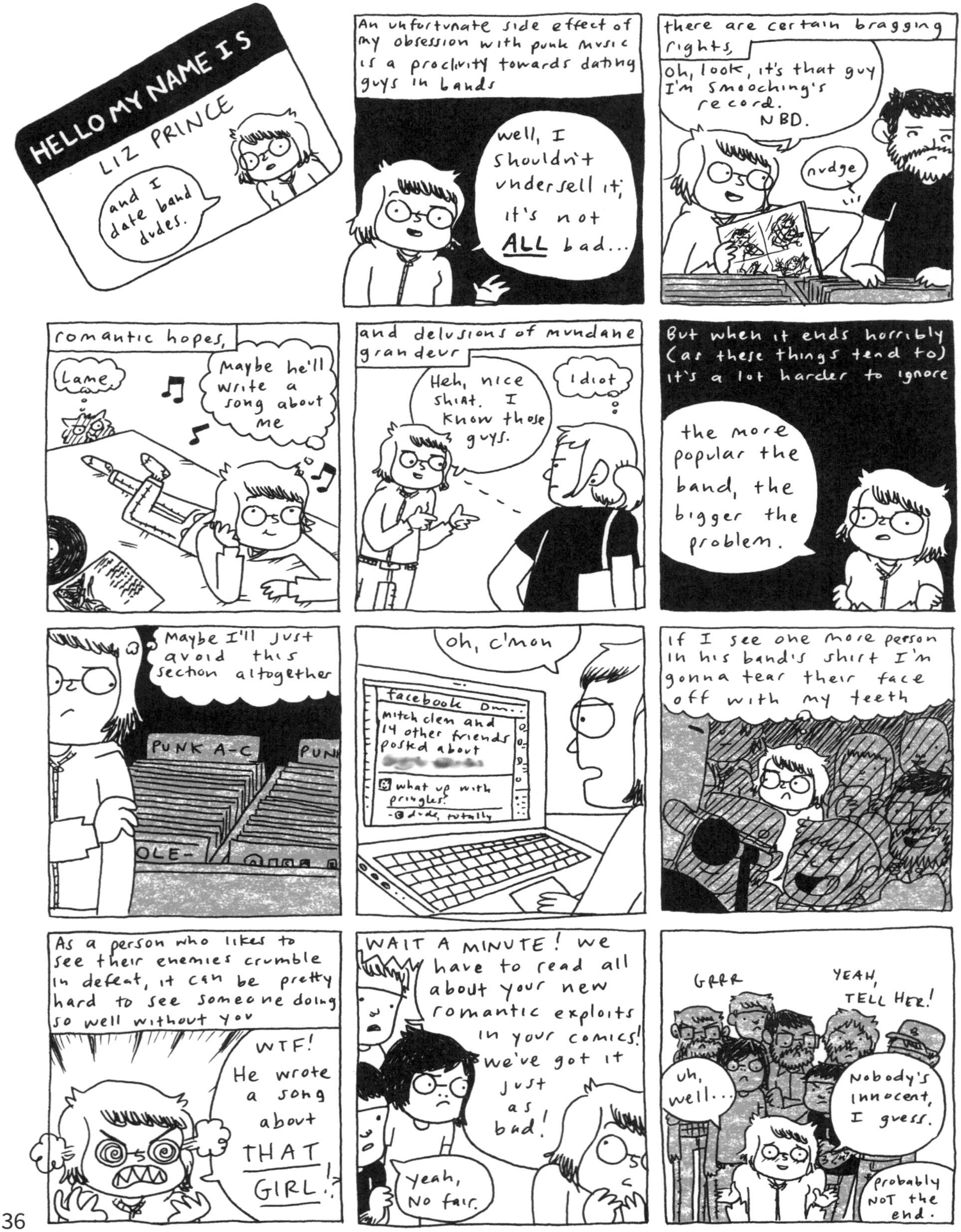
HELLO MY NAME IS
LIZ PRINCE
and I date band dudes.
An unfortunate side effect of my obsession with punk music is a proclivity towards dating guys in bands
well, I shouldn't undersell it; it's not ALL bad...
there are certain bragging rights,
Oh, look, it's that guy I'm smooching's record. NBD.
nudge
romantic hopes,
Lame.
Maybe he'll write a song about me
and delusions of mundane grandeur
Heh, nice shirt. I know those guys.
Idiot
But when it ends horribly (as these things tend to) it's a lot harder to ignore
the more popular the band, the bigger the problem.
Maybe I'll just avoid this section altogether
PUNK A-C
PUN
OLE-
oh, c'mon
facebook
mitch clem and 14 other friends posted about
what up with pringles?
dude, totally
If I see one more person in his band's shirt I'm gonna tear their face off with my teeth
As a person who likes to see their enemies crumble in defeat, it can be pretty hard to see someone doing so well without you
WTF! He wrote a song about THAT GIRL!?
WAIT A MINUTE! We have to read all about your new romantic exploits in your comics! We've got it just as bad!
yeah, No fair.
GRRR
YEAH, TELL HER!
uh, well...
Nobody's innocent, I guess.
probably NOT the end.

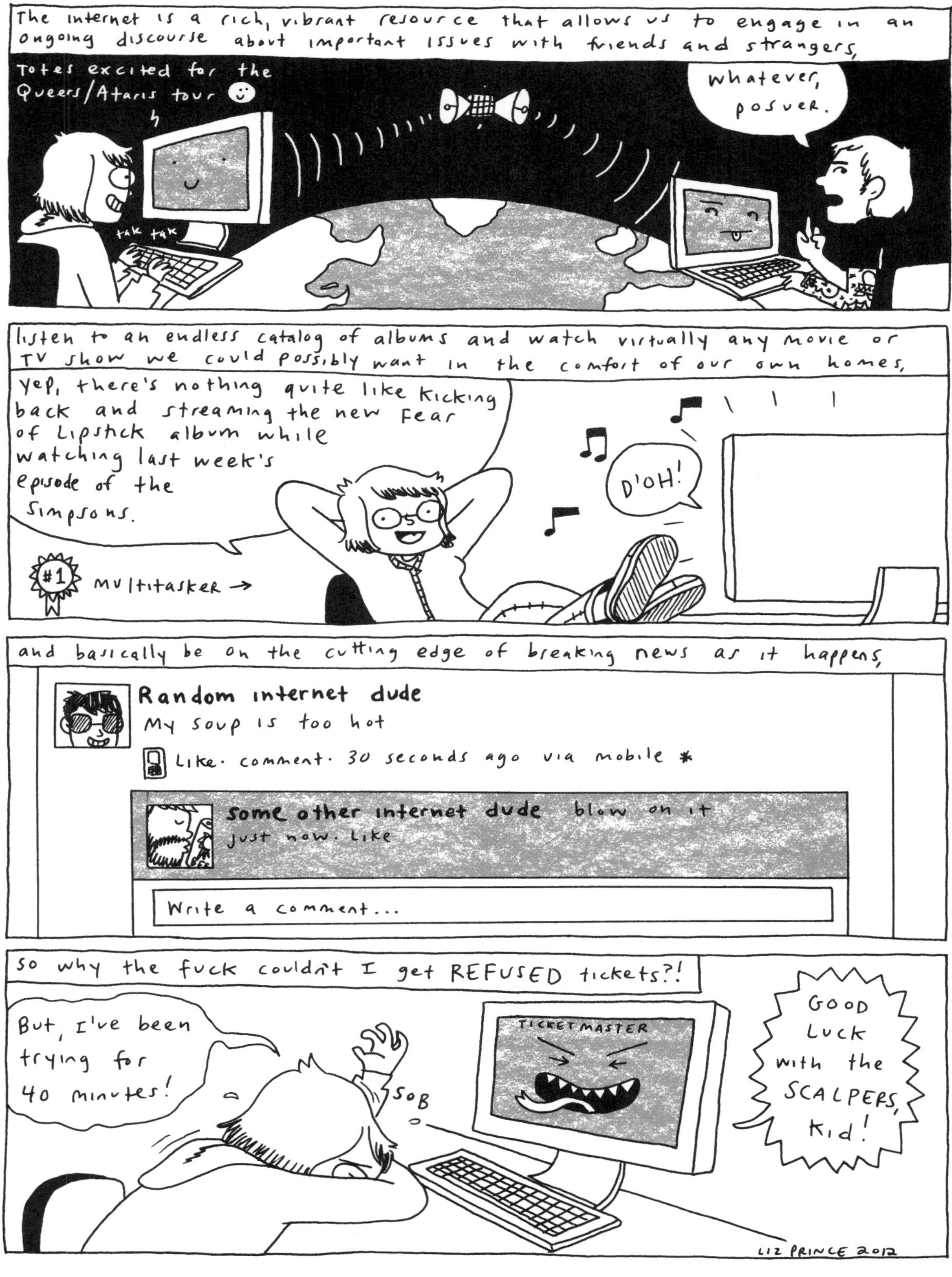
The internet is a rich, vibrant resource that allows us to engage in an ongoing discourse about important issues with friends and strangers,
Totes excited for the Queers/Ataris tour
whatever, posuer.
tak tak
listen to an endless catalog of albums and watch virtually any movie or TV show we could possibly want in the comfort of our own homes,
Yep, there's nothing quite like kicking back and streaming the new Fear of Lipstick album while watching last week's episode of the Simpsons.
D'OH!
#1
MULTITASKER →
and basically be on the cutting edge of breaking news as it happens,
Random internet dude
My soup is too hot
Like · comment · 30 seconds ago via mobile
Some other internet dude blow on it
just now · Like
Write a comment...
so why the fuck couldn't I get REFUSED tickets?!
But, I've been trying for 40 minutes!
SOB
TICKETMASTER
GOOD LUCK with the SCALPERS, Kid!
LIZ PRINCE 2012

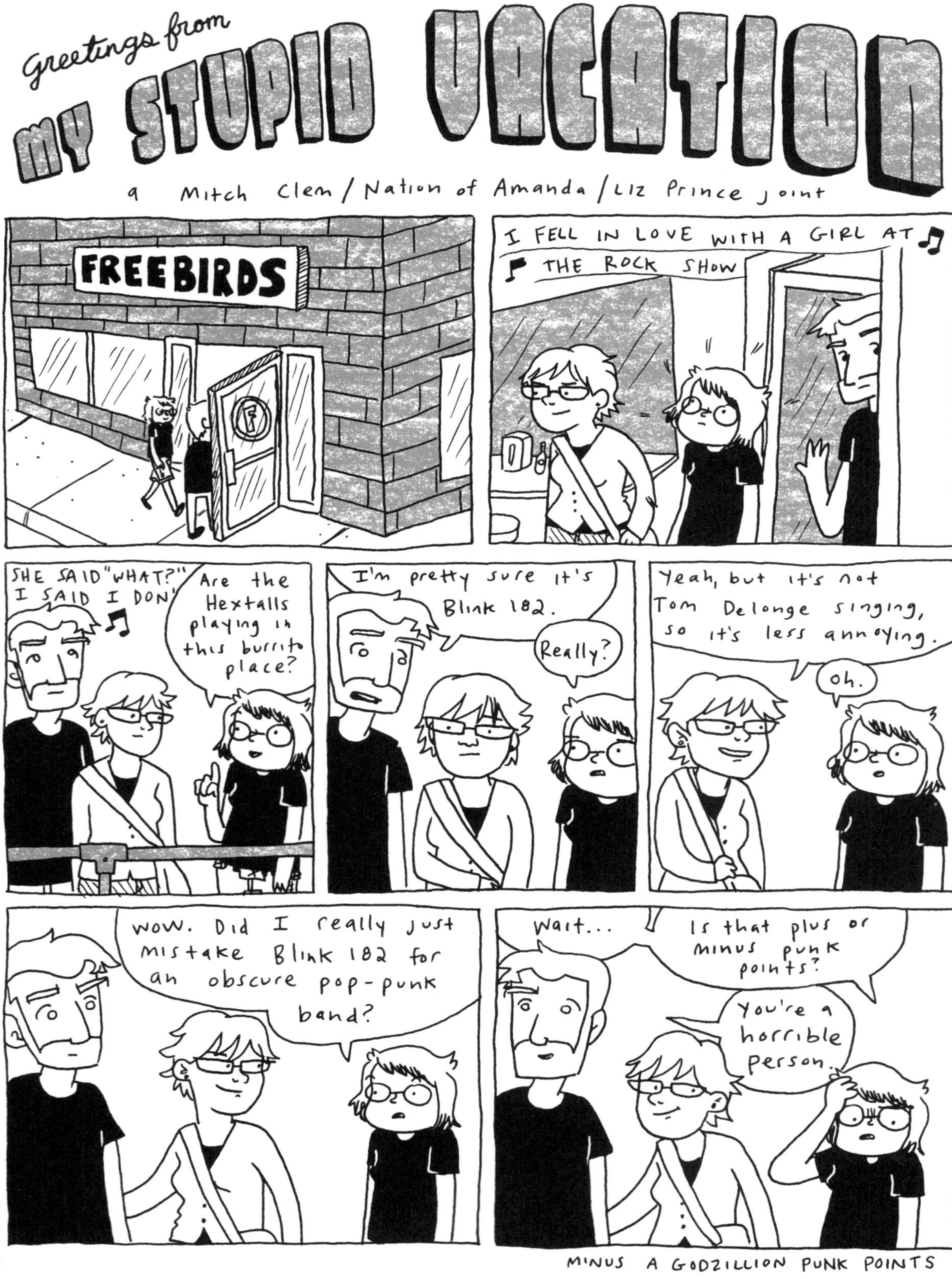
Greetings from
MY STUPID VACATION
a Mitch Clem / Nation of Amanda / Liz Prince joint
FREEBIRDS
I FELL IN LOVE WITH A GIRL AT THE ROCK SHOW
SHE SAID "WHAT?" I SAID I DON'
Are the Hextalls playing in this burrito place?
I'm pretty sure it's Blink 182.
Really?
Yeah, but it's not Tom Delonge singing, so it's less annoying.
oh.
wow. Did I really just mistake Blink 182 for an obscure pop-punk band?
Wait...
Is that plus or minus punk points?
You're a horrible person.
MINUS A GODZILLION PUNK POINTS

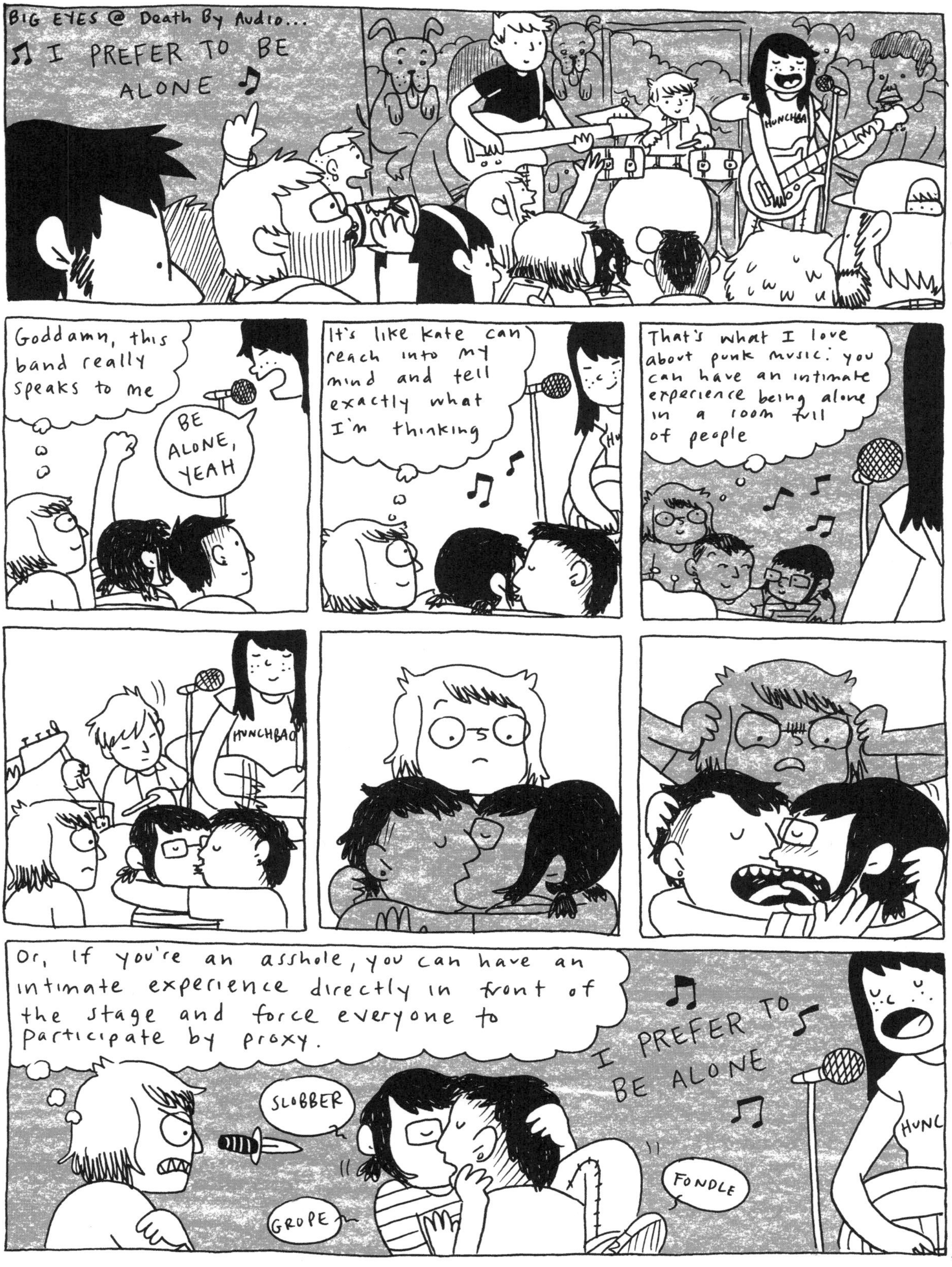
BIG EYES @ Death By Audio...
♫ I PREFER TO BE ALONE ♪
HUNCHBA
Goddamn, this band really speaks to me
BE ALONE, YEAH
It's like Kate can reach into my mind and tell exactly what I'm thinking
That's what I love about punk music: you can have an intimate experience being alone in a room full of people
HUNCHBAC
Or, if you're an asshole, you can have an intimate experience directly in front of the stage and force everyone to participate by proxy.
I PREFER TO BE ALONE
SLOBBER
GROPE
FONDLE
HUNC

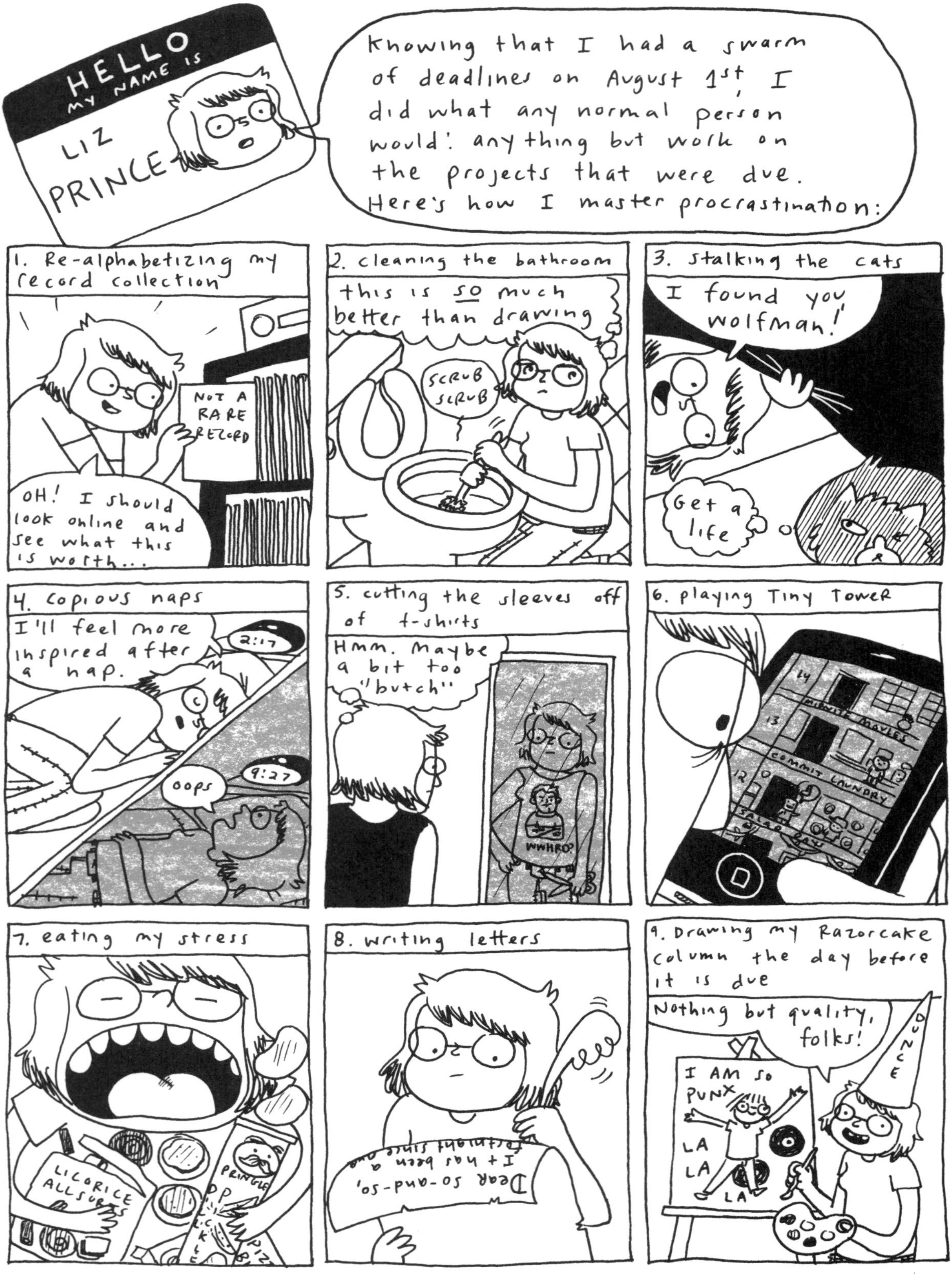
HELLO MY NAME IS
LIZ PRINCE
Knowing that I had a swarm of deadlines on August 1st, I did what any normal person would: anything but work on the projects that were due. Here's how I master procrastination:
1. Re-alphabetizing my record collection
NOT A RARE RECORD
OH! I should look online and see what this is worth...
2. cleaning the bathroom
this is SO much better than drawing
SCRUB SCRUB
3. Stalking the cats
I found you wolfman!
Get a life
4. copious naps
I'll feel more inspired after a nap.
2:17
9:27
oops
5. cutting the sleeves off of t-shirts
Hmm. Maybe a bit too "butch"
WWHRD?
6. playing Tiny Tower
MIDNITE MAYLES
COMMIT LAUNDRY
SALAD DAYS
7. eating my stress
LICORICE ALLSORTS
PRINGLES
8. writing letters
Dear so-and-so, It has been a fortnight since our
9. Drawing my Razorcake column the day before it is due
Nothing but quality, folks!
DUNCE
I AM SO PUNX
LA LA LA

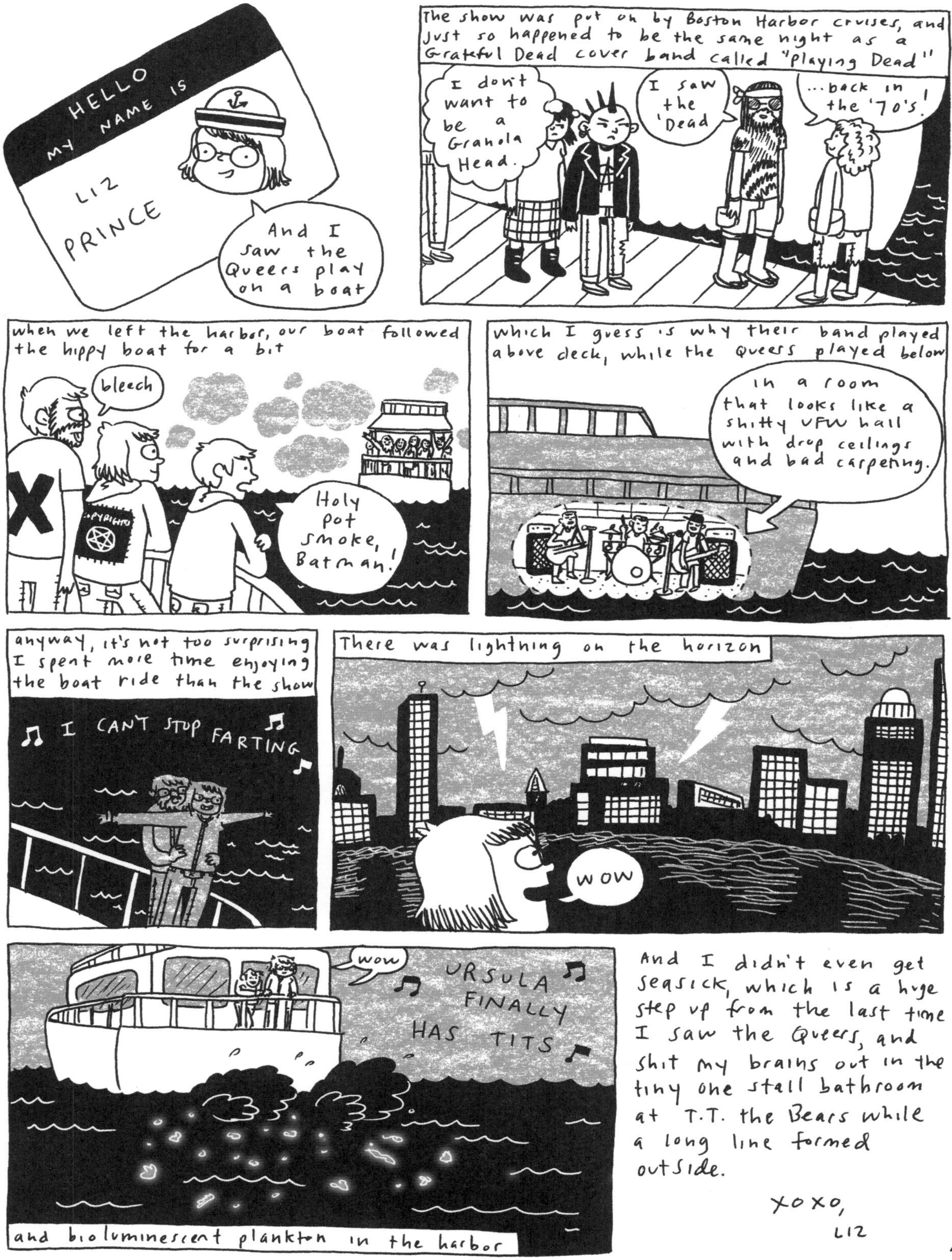
HELLO
MY NAME IS
LIZ
PRINCE
And I saw the Queers play on a boat
The show was put on by Boston Harbor cruises, and just so happened to be the same night as a Grateful Dead cover band called "Playing Dead"
I don't want to be a Granola Head.
I saw the 'Dead
...back in the '70's!
when we left the harbor, our boat followed the hippy boat for a bit
bleech
COPYRIGHTS
Holy pot smoke, Batman!
which I guess is why their band played above deck, while the Queers played below
in a room that looks like a shitty VFW hall with drop ceilings and bad carpeting.
anyway, it's not too surprising I spent more time enjoying the boat ride than the show
I CAN'T STOP FARTING
There was lightning on the horizon
WOW
WOW
URSULA FINALLY HAS TITS
and bioluminescent plankton in the harbor
And I didn't even get seasick, which is a huge step up from the last time I saw the Queers, and shit my brains out in the tiny one stall bathroom at T.T. the Bears while a long line formed outside.
xoxo,
LIZ

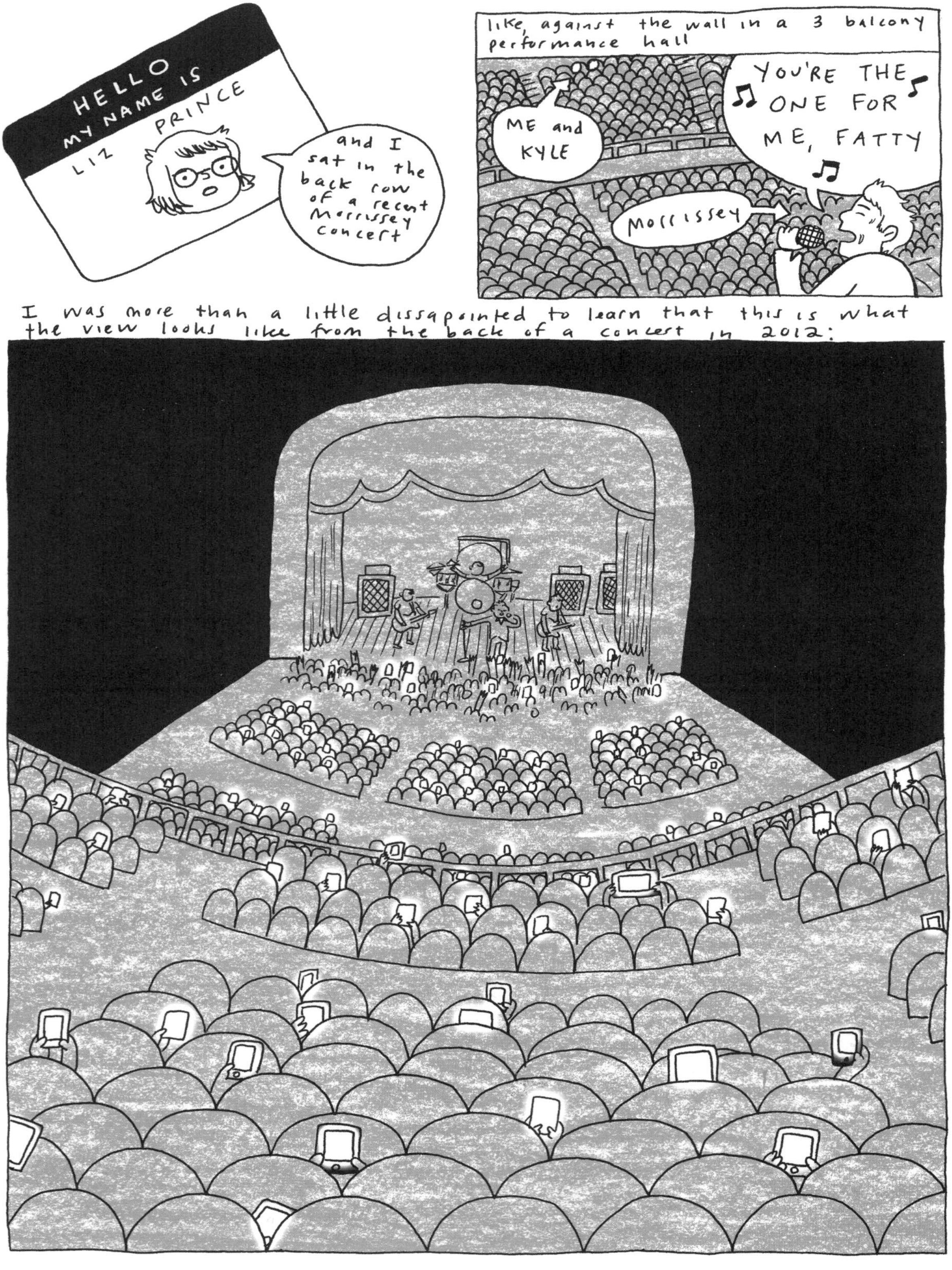
HELLO MY NAME IS
LIZ PRINCE
and I sat in the back row of a recent Morrissey concert
like, against the wall in a 3 balcony performance hall
ME and KYLE
YOU'RE THE ONE FOR ME, FATTY
Morrissey
I was more than a little dissapointed to learn that this is what the view looks like from the back of a concert in 2012:

PUNK ANATOMY 101 WITH PROFESSOR LIZ PRINCE 2013

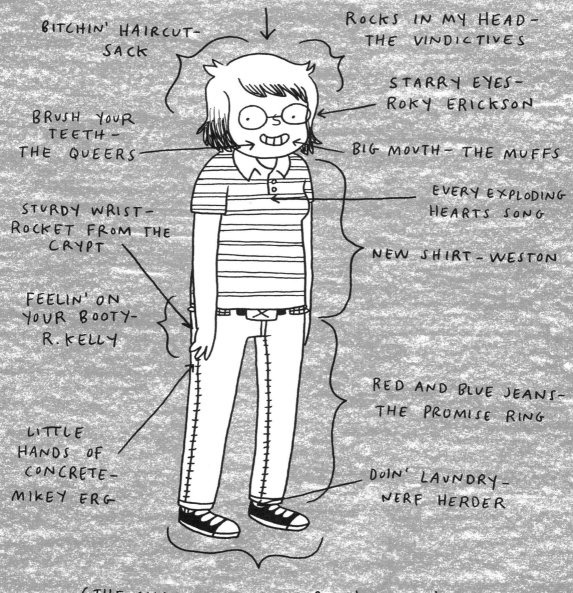

MY BRAIN IS HANGING UPSIDE DOWN (BONZO GOES TO BITBURG) —THE RAMONES

BITCHIN' HAIRCUT— SACK

ROCKS IN MY HEAD— THE VINDICTIVES

STARRY EYES— ROKY ERICKSON

BRUSH YOUR TEETH — THE QUEERS

BIG MOUTH— THE MUFFS

EVERY EXPLODING HEARTS SONG

STURDY WRIST— ROCKET FROM THE CRYPT

NEW SHIRT—WESTON

FEELIN' ON YOUR BOOTY— R. KELLY

RED AND BLUE JEANS— THE PROMISE RING

LITTLE HANDS OF CONCRETE— MIKEY ERG

DOIN' LAUNDRY— NERF HERDER

(THE ANGELS WANNA WEAR MY) RED SHOES— ELVIS COSTELLO

LIZ PRINCE PRESENTS A LIZ PRINCE SKILL SHARE

LIZ PRINCE'S GUIDE TO SPENDING TIME BY YOURSELF

Here's the 411: I know nobody wants to be LONELY but spending time by yourself because you WANT to can be super liberating

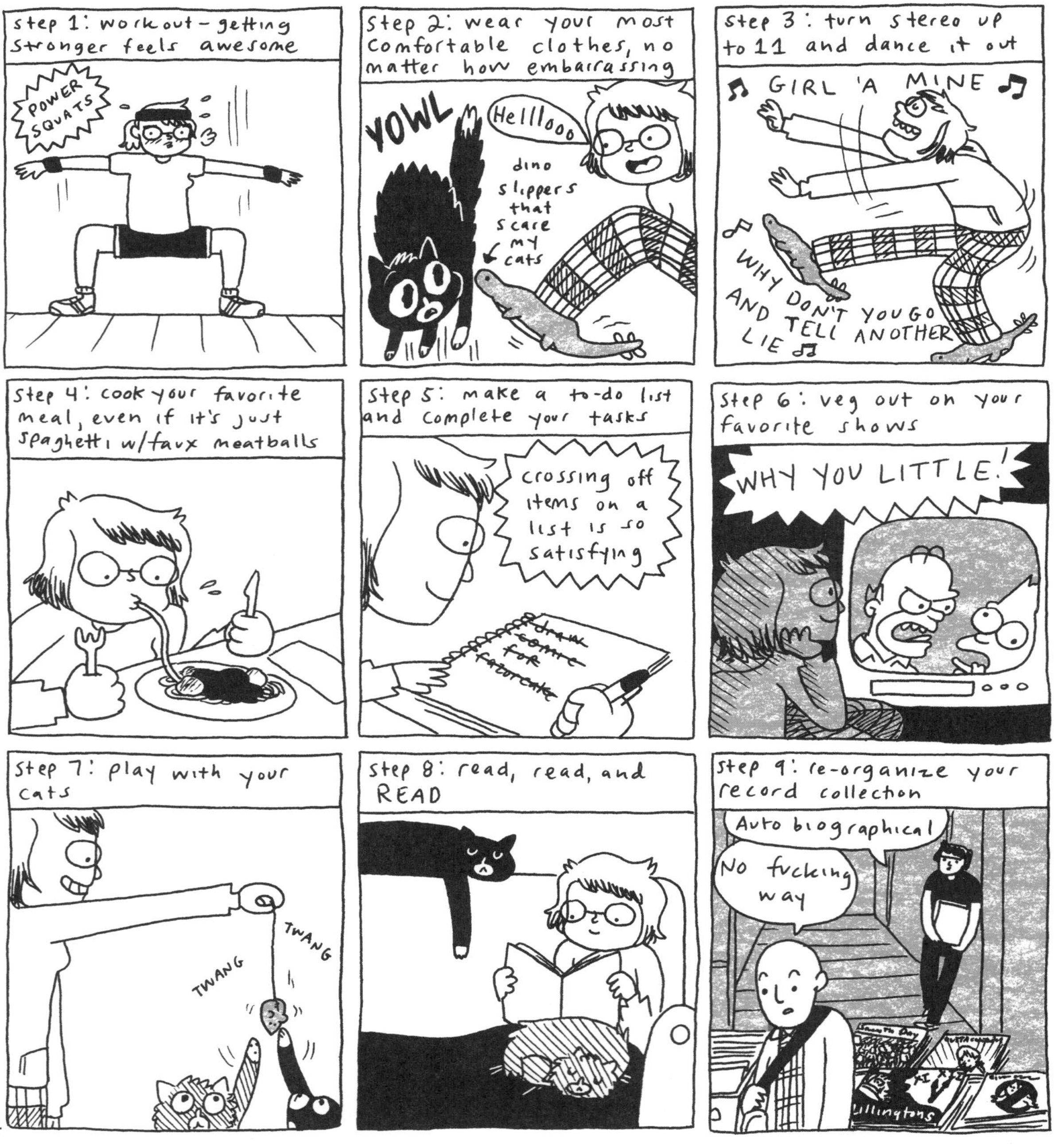
step 1: work out - getting stronger feels awesome
POWER SQUATS
step 2: wear your most comfortable clothes, no matter how embarrassing
YOWL
Hellllooo
dino slippers that scare my cats
step 3: turn stereo up to 11 and dance it out
♫ GIRL 'A MINE ♫
♪ WHY DON'T YOU GO AND TELL ANOTHER LIE ♫
step 4: cook your favorite meal, even if it's just spaghetti w/faux meatballs
step 5: make a to-do list and complete your tasks
crossing off items on a list is so satisfying
draw comic for faturcake
step 6: veg out on your favorite shows
WHY YOU LITTLE!
step 7: play with your cats
TWANG
TWANG
step 8: read, read, and READ
step 9: re-organize your record collection
Autobiographical
No fucking way

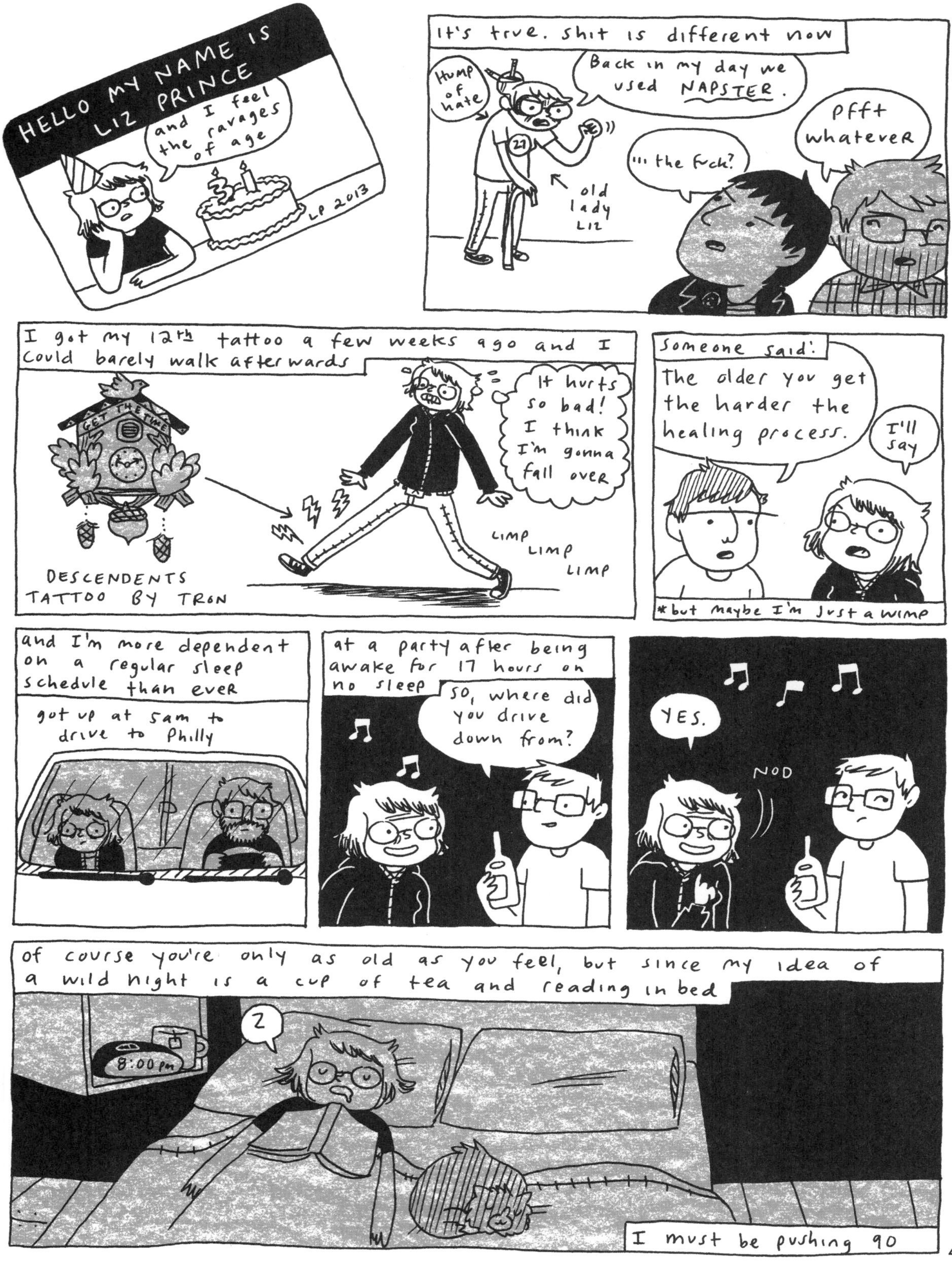
HELLO MY NAME IS LIZ PRINCE
and I feel the ravages of age
LP 2013
It's true. shit is different now
Hump of hate
Back in my day we used NAPSTER.
27
old lady Liz
... the fuck?
Pfft whatever
I got my 12th tattoo a few weeks ago and I could barely walk afterwards
GET THE TIME
DESCENDENTS TATTOO BY TRON
It hurts so bad! I think I'm gonna fall over
LIMP LIMP LIMP
Someone said:
The older you get the harder the healing process.
I'll say
*but maybe I'm just a wimp
and I'm more dependent on a regular sleep schedule than ever
got up at 5am to drive to Philly
at a party after being awake for 17 hours on no sleep
So, where did you drive down from?
YES.
NOD
of course you're only as old as you feel, but since my idea of a wild night is a cup of tea and reading in bed
Z
8:00pm
I must be pushing 90

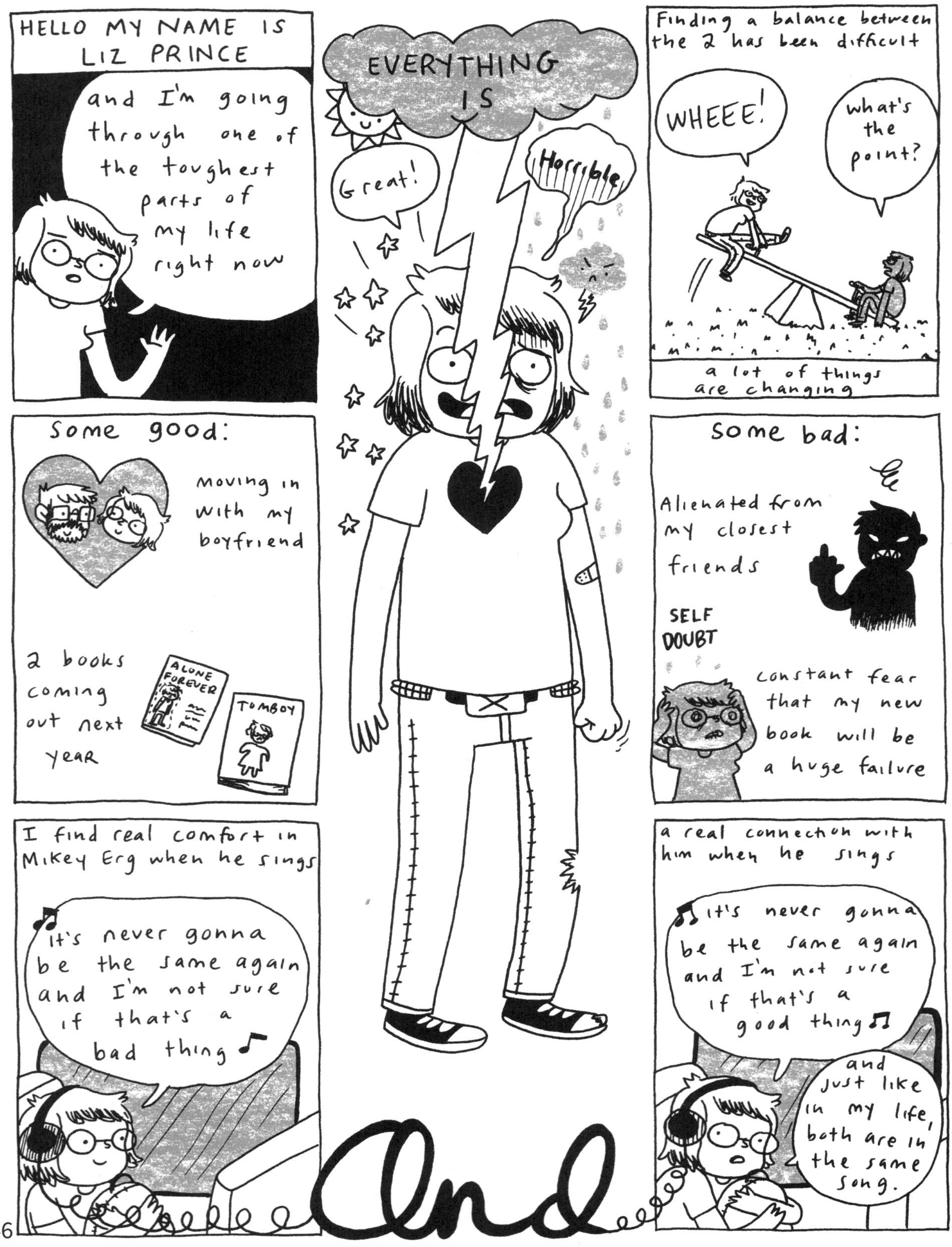

HELLO MY NAME IS LIZ PRINCE
and I'm going through one of the toughest parts of my life right now
EVERYTHING IS
Great!
Horrible
Finding a balance between the 2 has been difficult
WHEEE!
what's the point?
a lot of things are changing
some good:
moving in with my boyfriend
2 books coming out next year
ALONE FOREVER
TOMBOY
some bad:
Alienated from my closest friends
SELF DOUBT
constant fear that my new book will be a huge failure
I find real comfort in Mikey Erg when he sings
It's never gonna be the same again and I'm not sure if that's a bad thing
a real connection with him when he sings
it's never gonna be the same again and I'm not sure if that's a good thing
and just like in my life, both are in the same song.
and

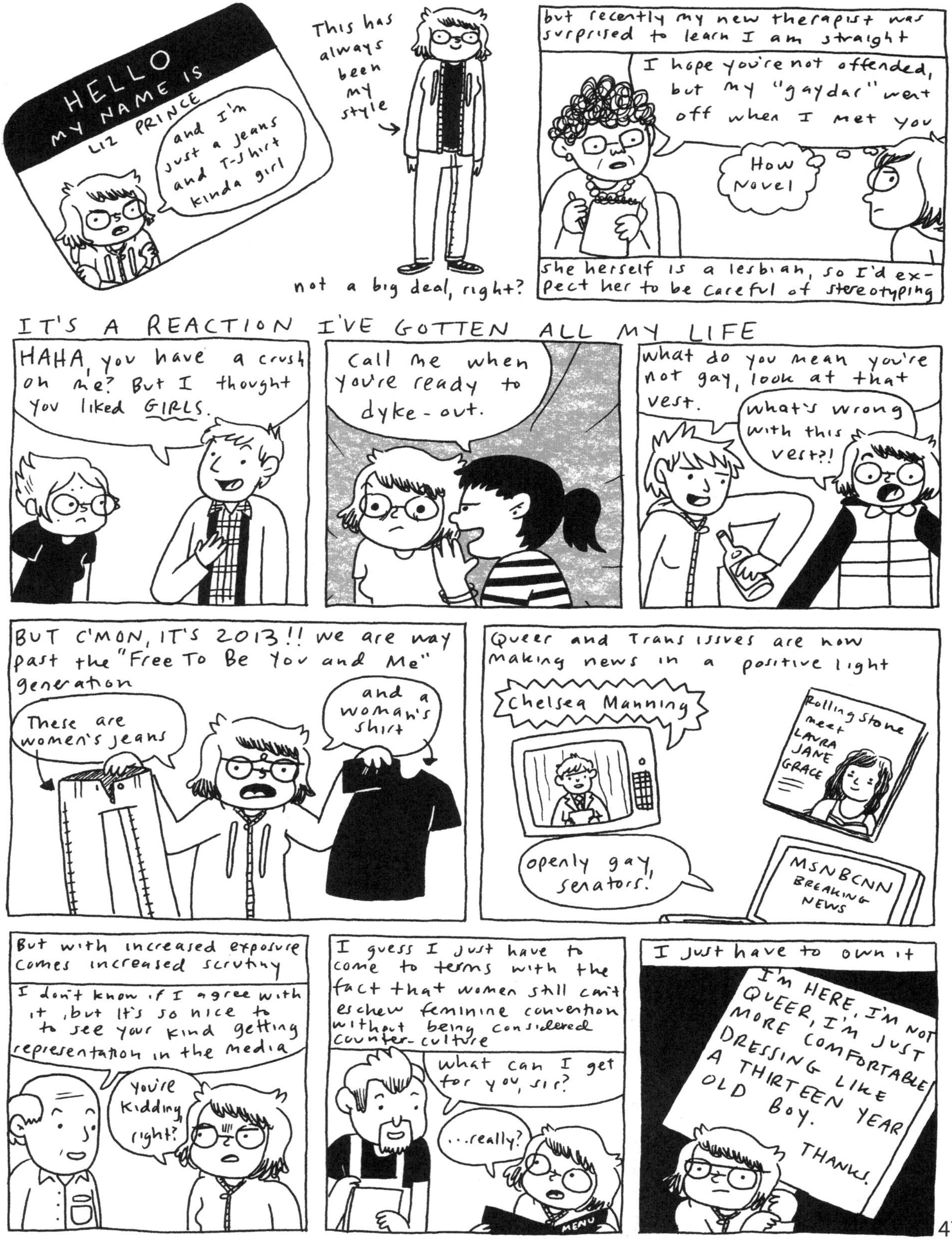
HELLO MY NAME IS
LIZ PRINCE
and I'm just a jeans and T-shirt kinda girl
This has always been my style
not a big deal, right?
but recently my new therapist was surprised to learn I am straight
I hope you're not offended, but my "gaydar" went off when I met you
How Novel
she herself is a lesbian, so I'd expect her to be careful of stereotyping
IT'S A REACTION I'VE GOTTEN ALL MY LIFE
HAHA, you have a crush on me? But I thought you liked GIRLS.
Call me when you're ready to dyke-out.
what do you mean you're not gay, look at that vest.
what's wrong with this vest?!
BUT C'MON, IT'S 2013!! we are way past the "Free To Be You and Me" generation
These are women's jeans
and a woman's shirt
Queer and Trans issues are now making news in a positive light
Chelsea Manning
Rolling Stone meet LAURA JANE GRACE
openly gay senators!
MSNBCNN BREAKING NEWS
But with increased exposure comes increased scrutiny
I don't know if I agree with it, but it's so nice to to see your kind getting representation in the media
You're kidding, right?
I guess I just have to come to terms with the fact that women still can't eschew feminine convention without being considered counter-culture
what can I get for you, sir?
...really?
MENU
I just have to own it
I'M HERE, I'M NOT QUEER, I'M JUST MORE COMFORTABLE DRESSING LIKE A THIRTEEN YEAR OLD BOY.
THANKS!

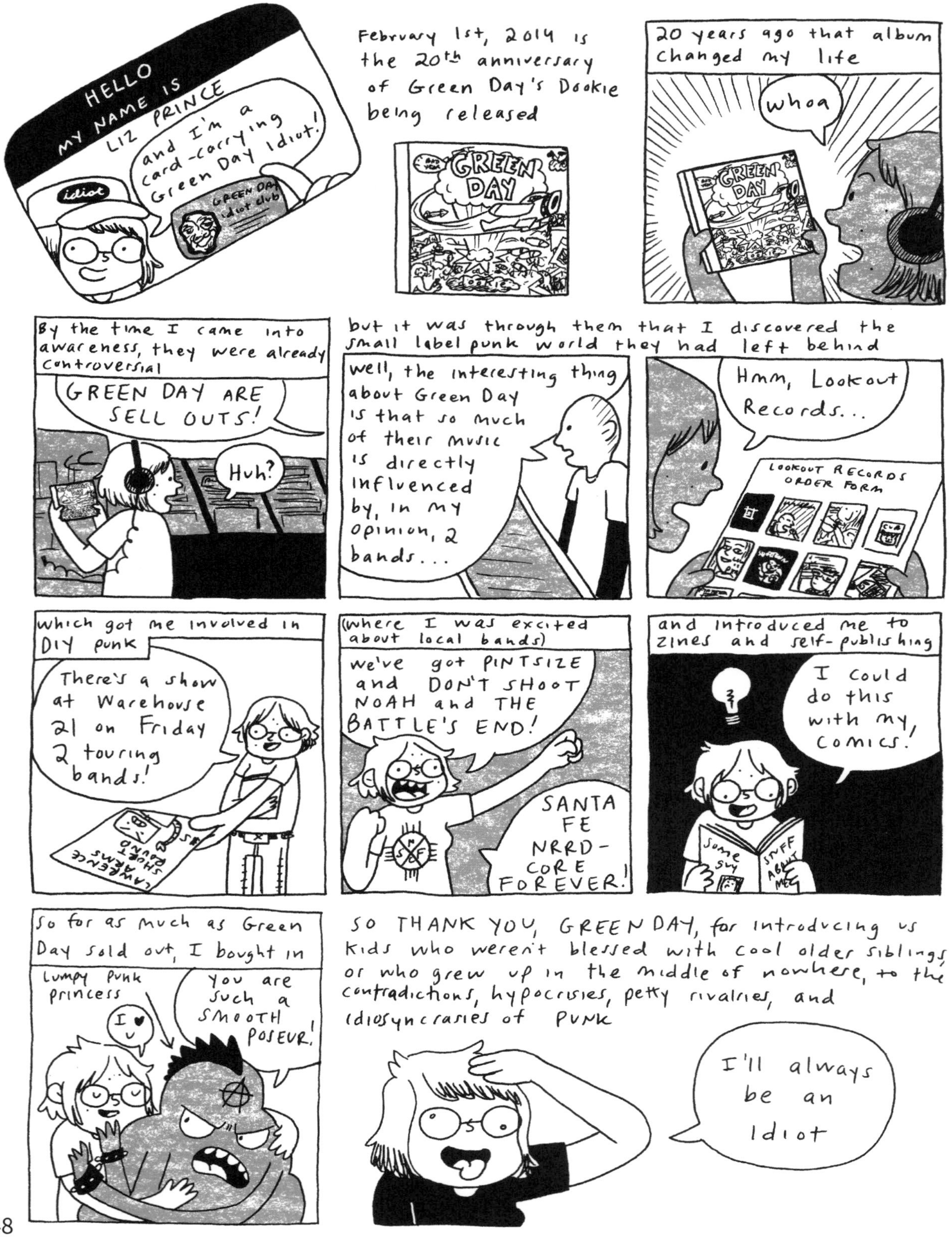
HELLO
MY NAME IS
LIZ PRINCE
and I'm a card-carrying Green Day Idiot!
idiot
GREEN DAY idiot club
February 1st, 2014 is the 20th anniversary of Green Day's Dookie being released
GREEN DAY
20 years ago that album changed my life
whoa
GREEN DAY
By the time I came into awareness, they were already controversial
GREEN DAY ARE SELL OUTS!
Huh?
but it was through them that I discovered the small label punk world they had left behind
well, the interesting thing about Green Day is that so much of their music is directly influenced by, in my opinion, 2 bands...
Hmm, Lookout Records...
LOOKOUT RECORDS ORDER FORM
which got me involved in DIY punk
There's a show at Warehouse 21 on Friday 2 touring bands!
(where I was excited about local bands)
we've got PINTSIZE and DON'T SHOOT NOAH and THE BATTLE'S END!
SANTA FE NRRD-CORE FOREVER!
and introduced me to zines and self-publishing
I could do this with my comics!
Some Guy
STUFF ABOUT ME
So for as much as Green Day sold out, I bought in
Lumpy Punk Princess
I ♥ U
You are such a SMOOTH POSEUR!
SO THANK YOU, GREEN DAY, for introducing us kids who weren't blessed with cool older siblings, or who grew up in the middle of nowhere, to the contradictions, hypocrisies, petty rivalries, and idiosyncrasies of PUNK
I'll always be an Idiot

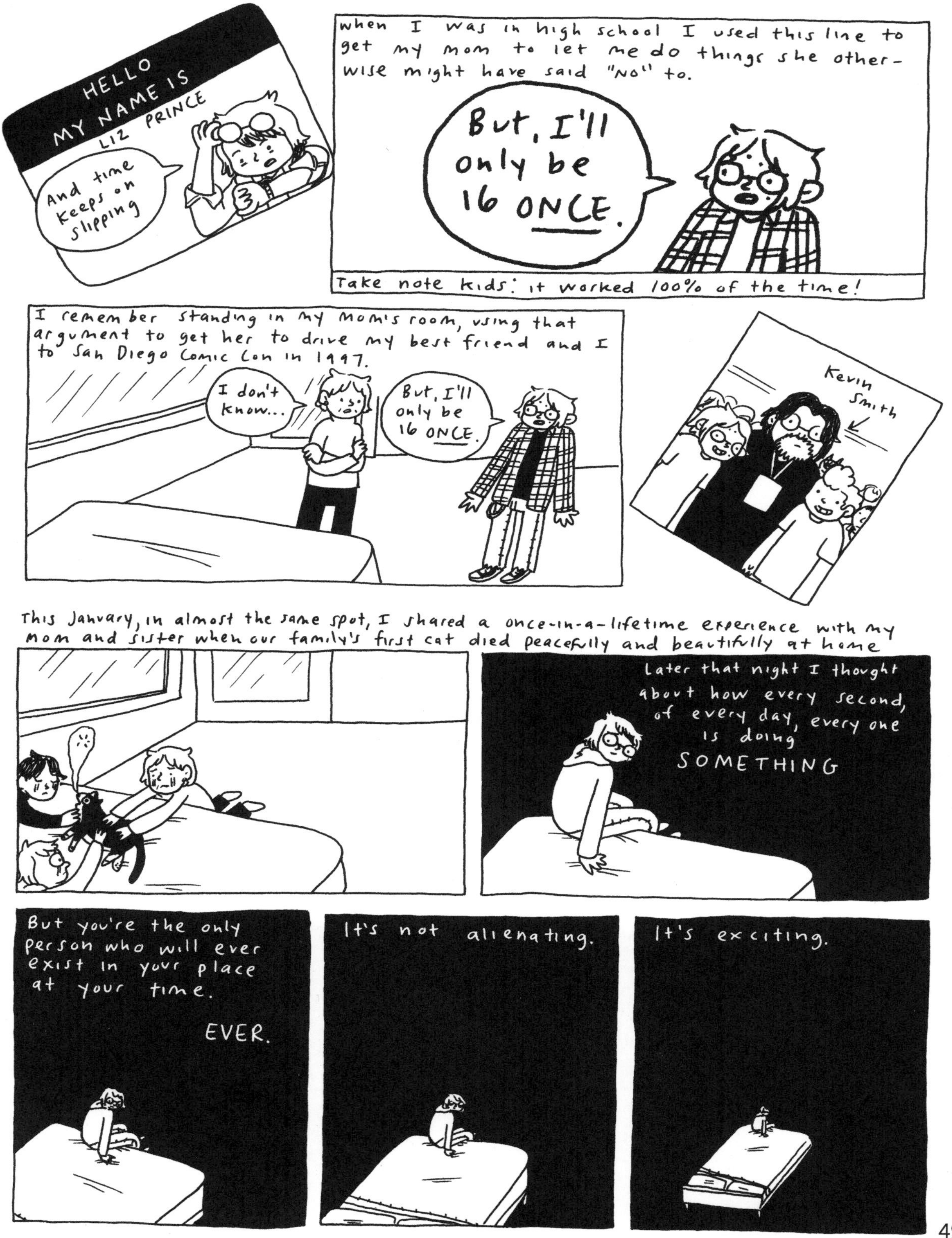
HELLO MY NAME IS
LIZ PRINCE
And time keeps on slipping
when I was in high school I used this line to get my mom to let me do things she otherwise might have said "NO" to.
But, I'll only be 16 ONCE.
Take note kids: it worked 100% of the time!
I remember standing in my Mom's room, using that argument to get her to drive my best friend and I to San Diego Comic Con in 1997.
I don't know...
But, I'll only be 16 ONCE.
Kevin Smith
This January, in almost the same spot, I shared a once-in-a-lifetime experience with my mom and sister when our family's first cat died peacefully and beautifully at home
Later that night I thought about how every second, of every day, every one is doing
SOMETHING
But you're the only person who will ever exist in your place at your time.
EVER.
It's not alienating.
It's exciting.

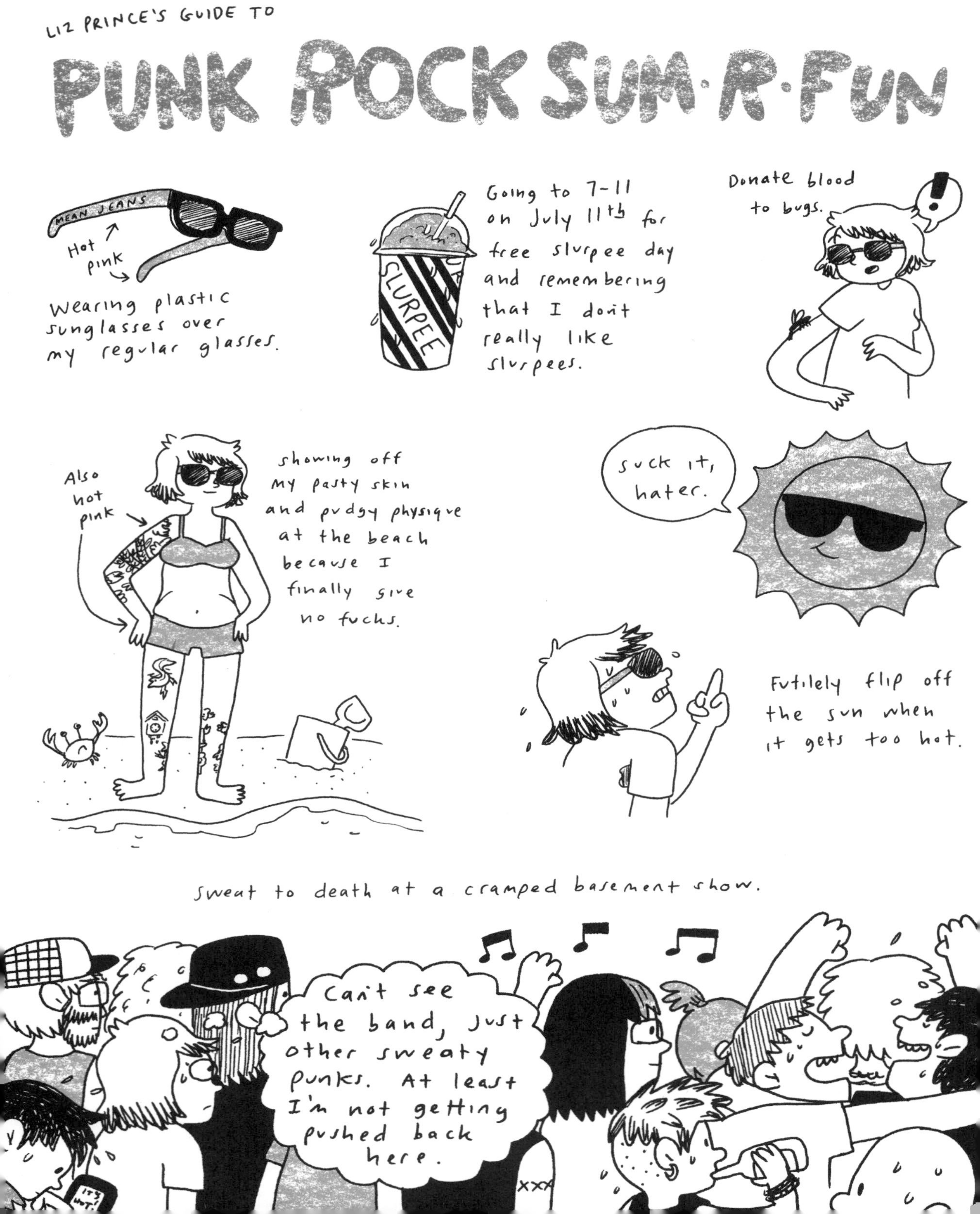
LIZ PRINCE'S GUIDE TO
PUNK ROCK SUM·R·FUN
MEAN JEANS
Hot pink
Wearing plastic sunglasses over my regular glasses.
SLURPEE
Going to 7-11 on July 11th for free slurpee day and remembering that I don't really like slurpees.
Donate blood to bugs.
!
Also hot pink
showing off my pasty skin and pudgy physique at the beach because I finally give no fucks.
suck it, hater.
Futilely flip off the sun when it gets too hot.
Sweat to death at a cramped basement show.
Can't see the band, just other sweaty punks. At least I'm not getting pushed back here.
IT'S HOT!
XXX

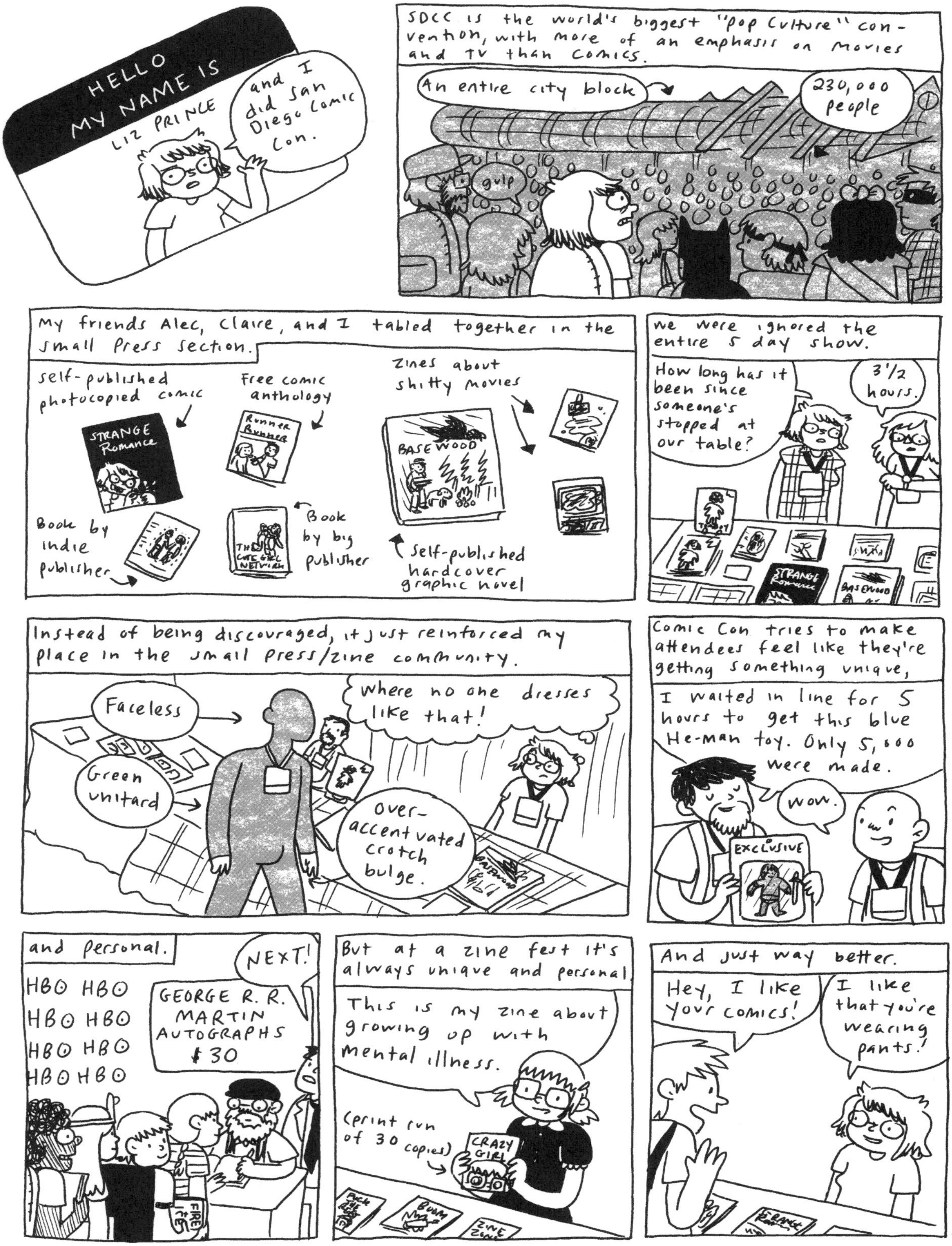
HELLO MY NAME IS
LIZ PRINCE
and I did San Diego Comic Con.
SDCC is the world's biggest "pop culture" convention, with more of an emphasis on movies and TV than comics.
An entire city block
230,000 people
gulp
My friends Alec, Claire, and I tabled together in the small press section.
self-published photocopied comic
STRANGE Romance
Free comic anthology
Runner Bubber
Zines about shitty movies
BASEWOOD
Book by indie publisher
Book by big publisher
THE CUTE GIRL NETWORK
Self-published hardcover graphic novel
We were ignored the entire 5 day show.
How long has it been since someone's stopped at our table?
3 1/2 hours.
STRANGE Romance
BASEWOOD
Instead of being discouraged, it just reinforced my place in the small press/zine community.
Faceless
Green unitard
Over-accentuated crotch bulge.
Where no one dresses like that!
BASEWOOD
Comic Con tries to make attendees feel like they're getting something unique,
I waited in line for 5 hours to get this blue He-man toy. Only 5,000 were made.
Wow.
EXCLUSIVE
and personal.
HBO HBO
HBO HBO
HBO HBO
HBO HBO
GEORGE R. R. MARTIN AUTOGRAPHS $30
NEXT!
FIRE
But at a zine fest it's always unique and personal.
This is my zine about growing up with mental illness.
(print run of 30 copies)
CRAZY GIRL
BOOM
ZINE
And just way better.
Hey, I like your comics!
I like that you're wearing pants!

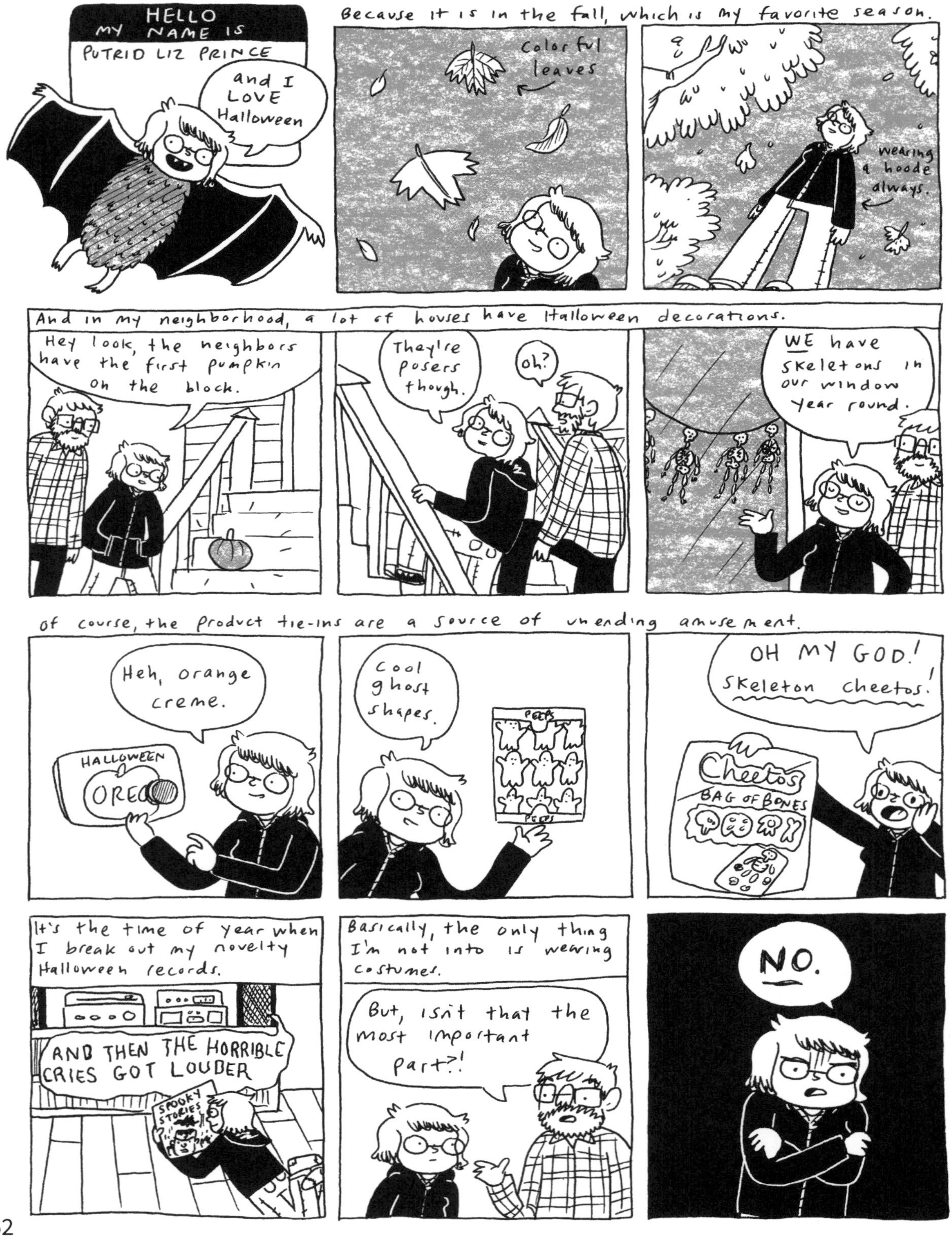

HELLO MY NAME IS
PUTRID LIZ PRINCE
and I LOVE Halloween
Because it is in the fall, which is my favorite season.
Colorful leaves
wearing a hoodie always.
And in my neighborhood, a lot of houses have Halloween decorations.
Hey look, the neighbors have the first pumpkin on the block.
They're posers though.
oh?
WE have skeletons in our window year round.
of course, the product tie-ins are a source of unending amusement.
Heh, orange creme.
HALLOWEEN OREO
Cool ghost shapes.
PEEPS
OH MY GOD! Skeleton cheetos!
Cheetos BAG OF BONES
It's the time of year when I break out my novelty Halloween records.
AND THEN THE HORRIBLE CRIES GOT LOUDER
SPOOKY STORIES
Basically, the only thing I'm not into is wearing costumes.
But, isn't that the most important part?!
NO.

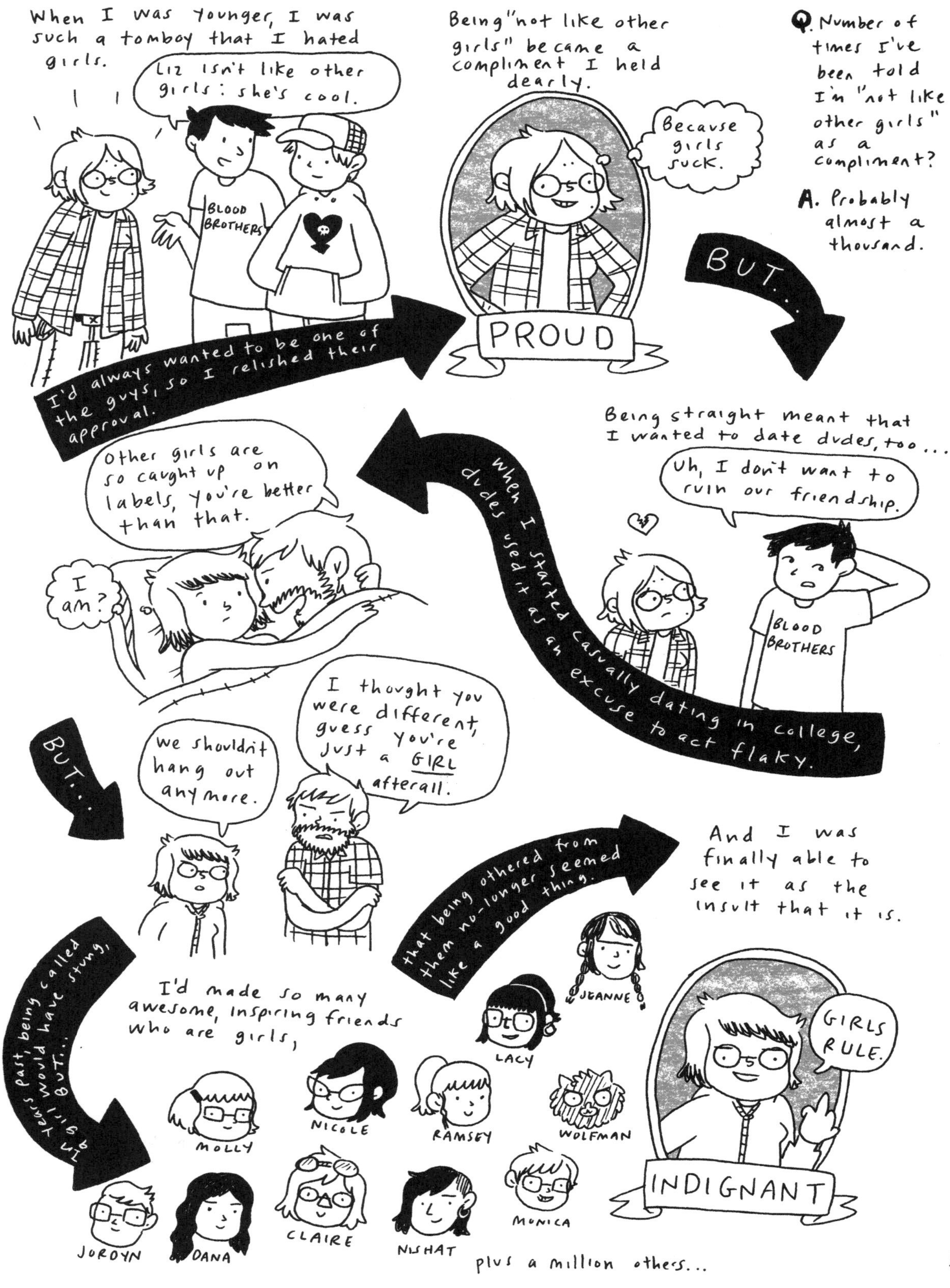
When I was younger, I was such a tomboy that I hated girls.
Liz isn't like other girls: she's cool.
BLOOD BROTHERS
I'd always wanted to be one of the guys, so I relished their approval.
Being "not like other girls" became a compliment I held dearly.
Because girls suck.
PROUD
Q. Number of times I've been told I'm "not like other girls" as a compliment?
A. Probably almost a thousand.
BUT...
Being straight meant that I wanted to date dudes, too...
Uh, I don't want to ruin our friendship.
BLOOD BROTHERS
When I started casually dating in college, dudes used it as an excuse to act flaky.
Other girls are so caught up on labels, you're better than that.
I am?
BUT...
We shouldn't hang out anymore.
I thought you were different, guess you're just a GIRL afterall.
In years past, being called a girl would have stung, BUT...
that being othered from them no-longer seemed like a good thing.
And I was finally able to see it as the insult that it is.
I'd made so many awesome, inspiring friends who are girls,
JEANNE
LACY
MOLLY
NICOLE
RAMSEY
WOLFMAN
JORDYN
DANA
CLAIRE
NISHAT
MONICA
GIRLS RULE.
INDIGNANT
plus a million others...

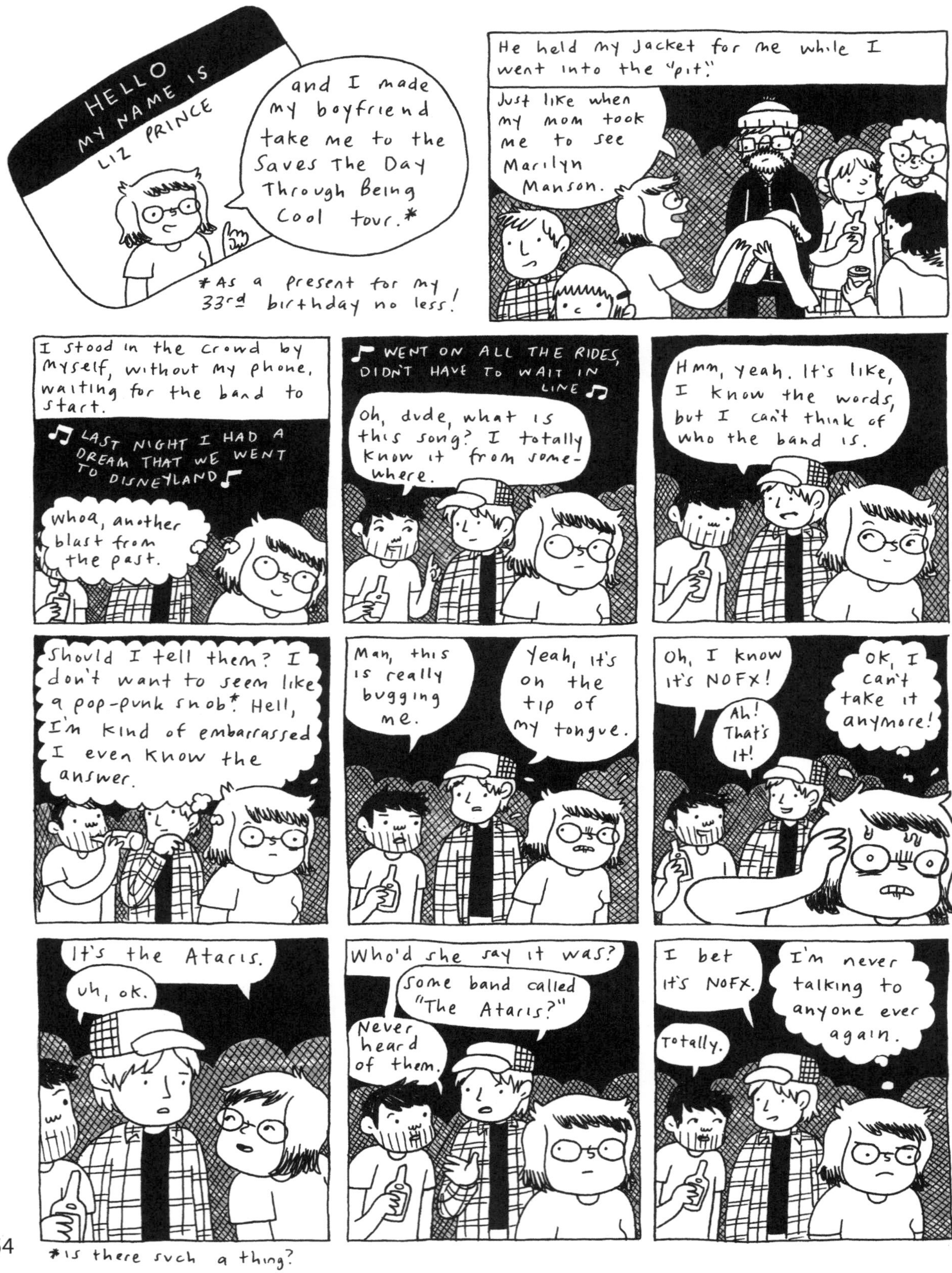
HELLO MY NAME IS
LIZ PRINCE
and I made my boyfriend take me to the Saves The Day Through Being Cool tour.*
*As a present for my 33rd birthday no less!
He held my jacket for me while I went into the "pit."
Just like when my mom took me to see Marilyn Manson.
I stood in the crowd by myself, without my phone, waiting for the band to start.
LAST NIGHT I HAD A DREAM THAT WE WENT TO DISNEYLAND
Whoa, another blast from the past.
WENT ON ALL THE RIDES, DIDN'T HAVE TO WAIT IN LINE
Oh, dude, what is this song? I totally know it from somewhere.
Hmm, yeah. It's like, I know the words, but I can't think of who the band is.
Should I tell them? I don't want to seem like a pop-punk snob*. Hell, I'm kind of embarrassed I even know the answer.
Man, this is really bugging me.
Yeah, it's on the tip of my tongue.
Oh, I know it's NOFX!
Ah! That's it!
OK, I can't take it anymore!
It's the Ataris.
Uh, ok.
Who'd she say it was?
Some band called "The Ataris?"
Never heard of them.
I bet it's NOFX.
Totally.
I'm never talking to anyone ever again.
*Is there such a thing?

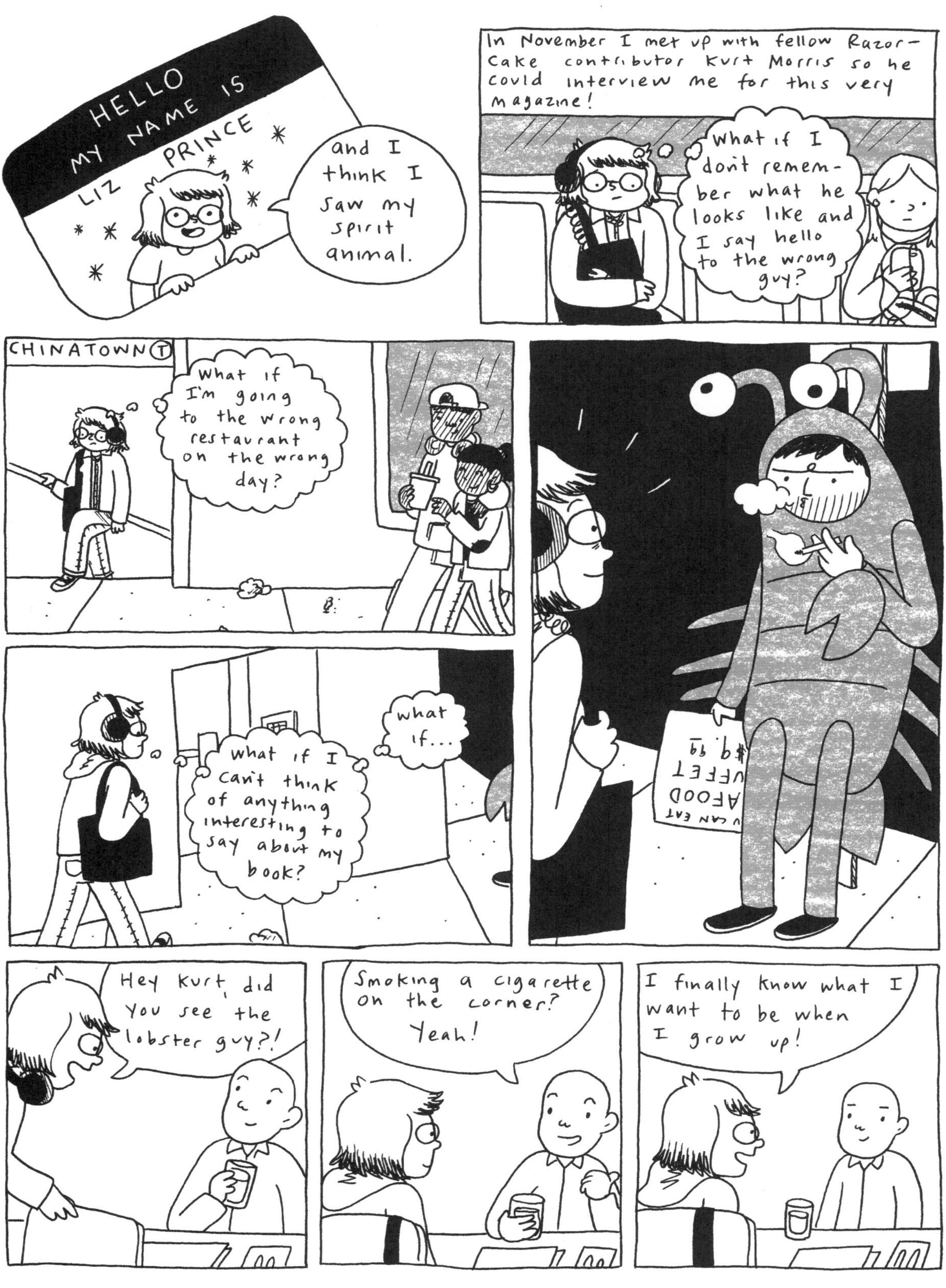
HELLO
MY NAME IS
LIZ PRINCE
and I think I saw my spirit animal.
In November I met up with fellow Razor-Cake contributor Kurt Morris so he could interview me for this very magazine!
What if I don't remember what he looks like and I say hello to the wrong guy?
CHINATOWN T
What if I'm going to the wrong restaurant on the wrong day?
what if I can't think of anything interesting to say about my book?
what if...
Hey Kurt, did you see the lobster guy?!
Smoking a cigarette on the corner?
Yeah!
I finally know what I want to be when I grow up!

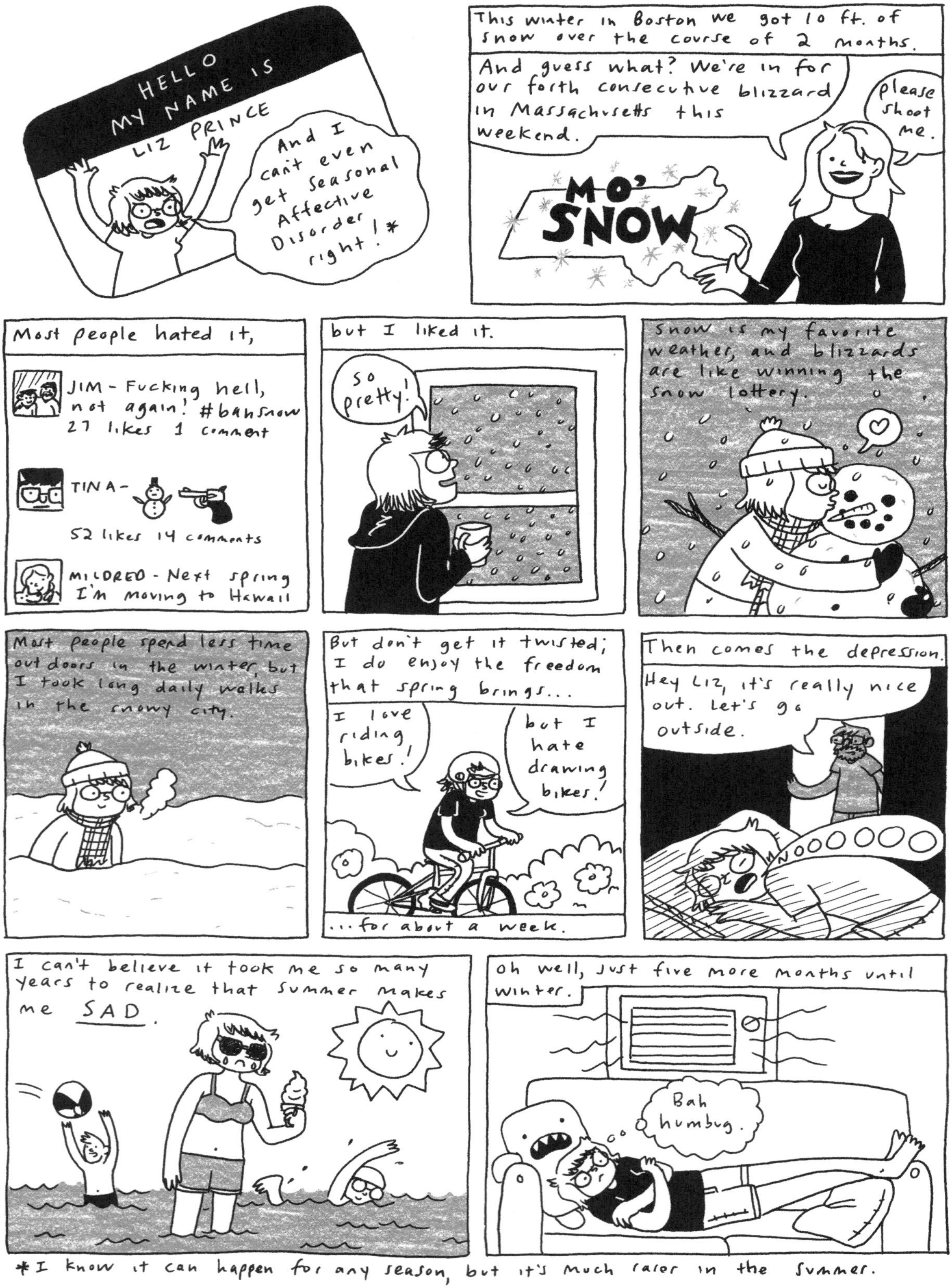
HELLO MY NAME IS
LIZ PRINCE
And I can't even get Seasonal Affective Disorder right! *
This winter in Boston we got 10 ft. of snow over the course of 2 months.
And guess what? We're in for our forth consecutive blizzard in Massachusetts this weekend.
MO' SNOW
please shoot me.
Most people hated it,
JIM - Fucking hell, not again! #bansnow
27 likes 1 comment
TINA -
52 likes 14 comments
MILDRED - Next spring I'm moving to Hawaii
but I liked it.
so pretty!
Snow is my favorite weather, and blizzards are like winning the snow lottery.
Most people spend less time outdoors in the winter, but I took long daily walks in the snowy city.
But don't get it twisted; I do enjoy the freedom that spring brings...
I love riding bikes!
but I hate drawing bikes!
...for about a week.
Then comes the depression.
Hey Liz, it's really nice out. Let's go outside.
NOOOOOO
I can't believe it took me so many years to realize that summer makes me SAD.
Oh well, just five more months until winter.
Bah humbug.

*I know it can happen for any season, but it's much rarer in the summer.

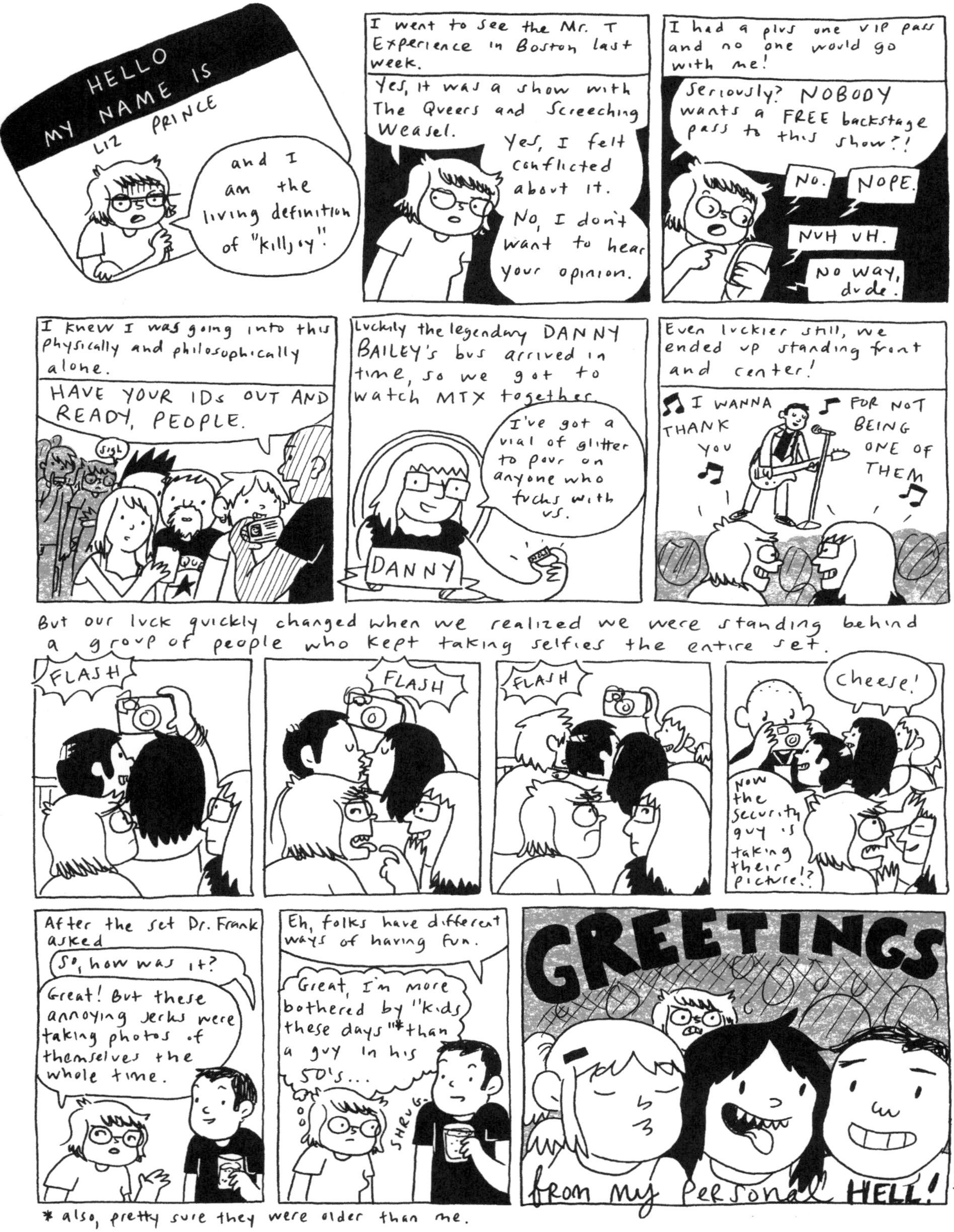
HELLO MY NAME IS
LIZ PRINCE
and I am the living definition of "killjoy".
I went to see the Mr. T Experience in Boston last week.
Yes, it was a show with The Queers and Screeching Weasel.
Yes, I felt conflicted about it.
No, I don't want to hear your opinion.
I had a plus one VIP pass and no one would go with me!
Seriously? NOBODY wants a FREE backstage pass to this show?!
No.
NOPE.
NUH UH.
No way, dude.
I knew I was going into this physically and philosophically alone.
HAVE YOUR IDs OUT AND READY, PEOPLE.
sigh
Luckily the legendary DANNY BAILEY's bus arrived in time, so we got to watch MTX together.
I've got a vial of glitter to pour on anyone who fucks with us.
DANNY
Even luckier still, we ended up standing front and center!
I WANNA THANK YOU FOR NOT BEING ONE OF THEM
But our luck quickly changed when we realized we were standing behind a group of people who kept taking selfies the entire set.
FLASH
FLASH
FLASH
Cheese!
Now the security guy is taking their picture!?
After the set Dr. Frank asked
So, how was it?
Great! But these annoying jerks were taking photos of themselves the whole time.
Eh, folks have different ways of having fun.
Great, I'm more bothered by "kids these days"* than a guy in his 50's...
SHRUG
GREETINGS from my personal HELL!
www.lizprincepower.com
* also, pretty sure they were older than me.

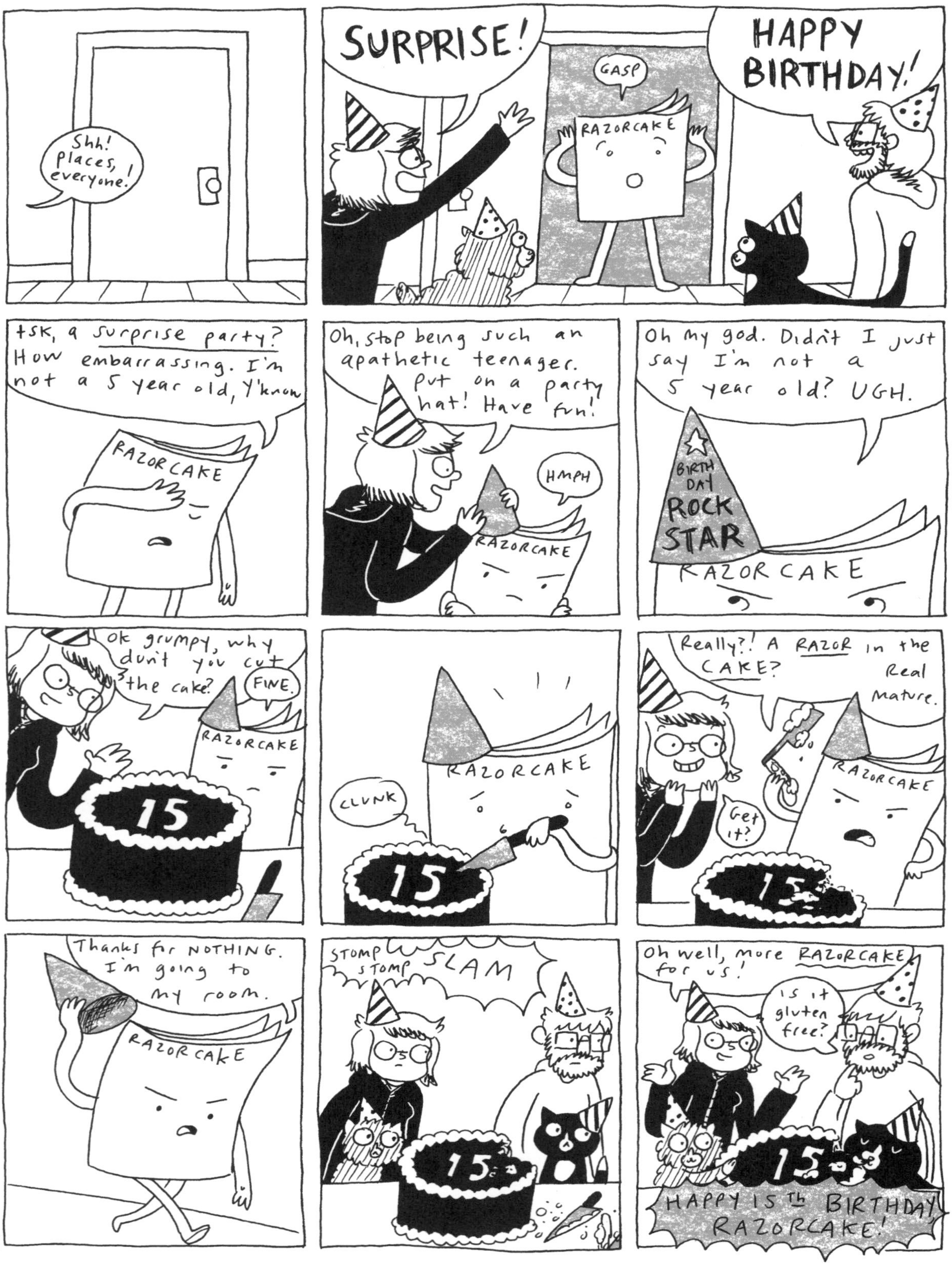
Shh! places, everyone!
SURPRISE!
GASP
RAZORCAKE
HAPPY BIRTHDAY!
tsk, a surprise party? How embarrassing. I'm not a 5 year old, Y'know
RAZORCAKE
Oh, stop being such an apathetic teenager. Put on a party hat! Have fun!
HMPH
RAZORCAKE
Oh my god. Didn't I just say I'm not a 5 year old? UGH.
BIRTH DAY ROCK STAR
RAZORCAKE
Ok grumpy, why don't you cut the cake?
FINE.
RAZORCAKE
15
CLUNK
RAZORCAKE
15
Really?! A RAZOR in the CAKE? Real mature.
Get it?
RAZORCAKE
Thanks for NOTHING. I'm going to my room.
RAZORCAKE
STOMP STOMP SLAM
15
Oh well, more RAZORCAKE for us!
Is it gluten free?
15
HAPPY 15TH BIRTHDAY RAZORCAKE!

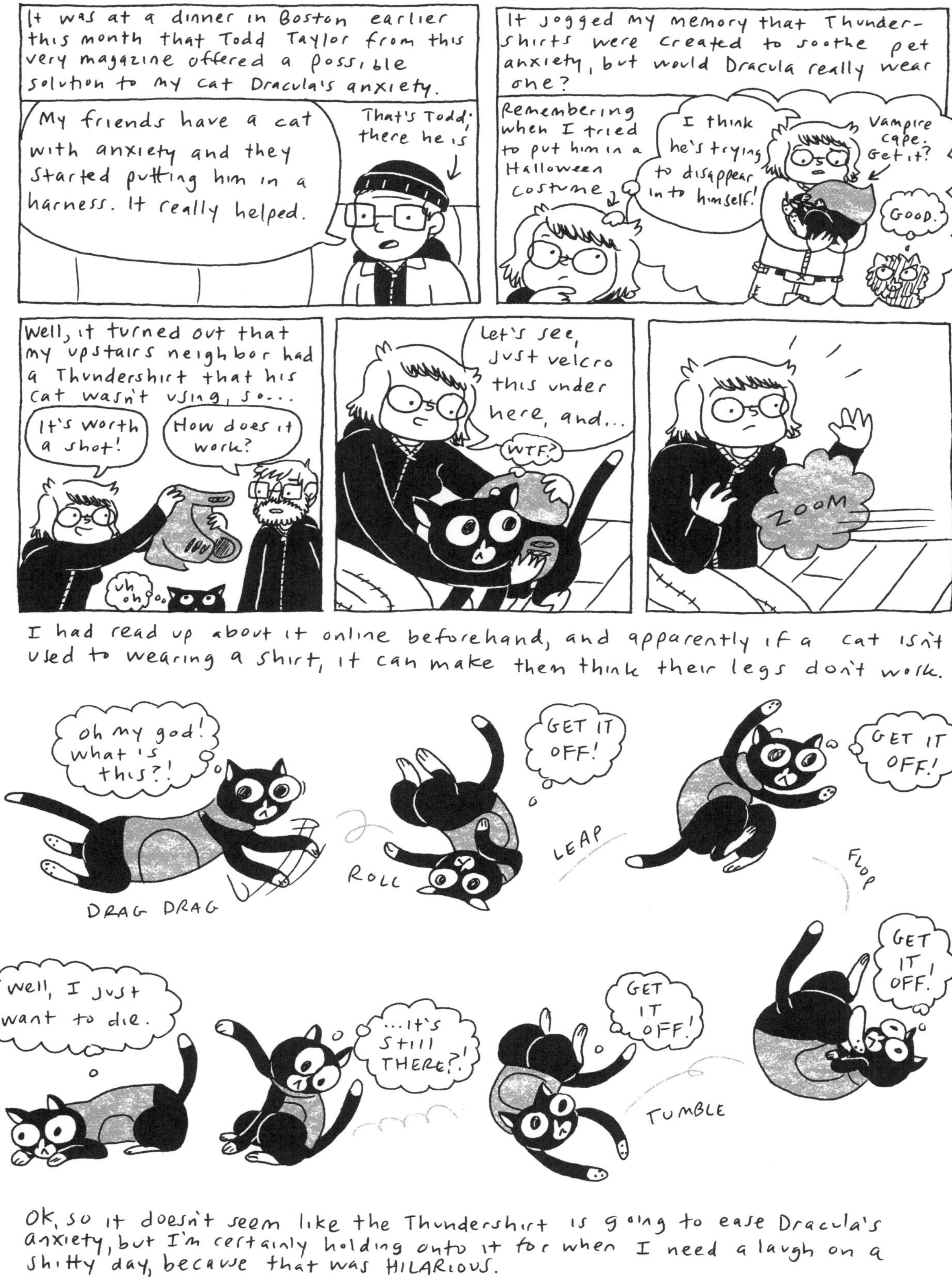
It was at a dinner in Boston earlier this month that Todd Taylor from this very magazine offered a possible solution to my cat Dracula's anxiety.
My friends have a cat with anxiety and they started putting him in a harness. It really helped.
That's Todd; there he is
It jogged my memory that Thundershirts were created to soothe pet anxiety, but would Dracula really wear one?
Remembering when I tried to put him in a Halloween costume
I think he's trying to disappear into himself!
Vampire cape. Get it?
GOOD.
Well, it turned out that my upstairs neighbor had a Thundershirt that his cat wasn't using, so...
It's worth a shot!
How does it work?
uh oh
Let's see, just velcro this under here, and...
WTF?
ZOOM
I had read up about it online beforehand, and apparently if a cat isn't used to wearing a shirt, it can make them think their legs don't work.
oh my god! what is this?!
DRAG DRAG
GET IT OFF!
ROLL
LEAP
GET IT OFF!
FLOP
GET IT OFF!
TUMBLE
GET IT OFF!
...it's still THERE?!
Well, I just want to die.
Ok, so it doesn't seem like the Thundershirt is going to ease Dracula's anxiety, but I'm certainly holding onto it for when I need a laugh on a shitty day, because that was HILARIOUS.

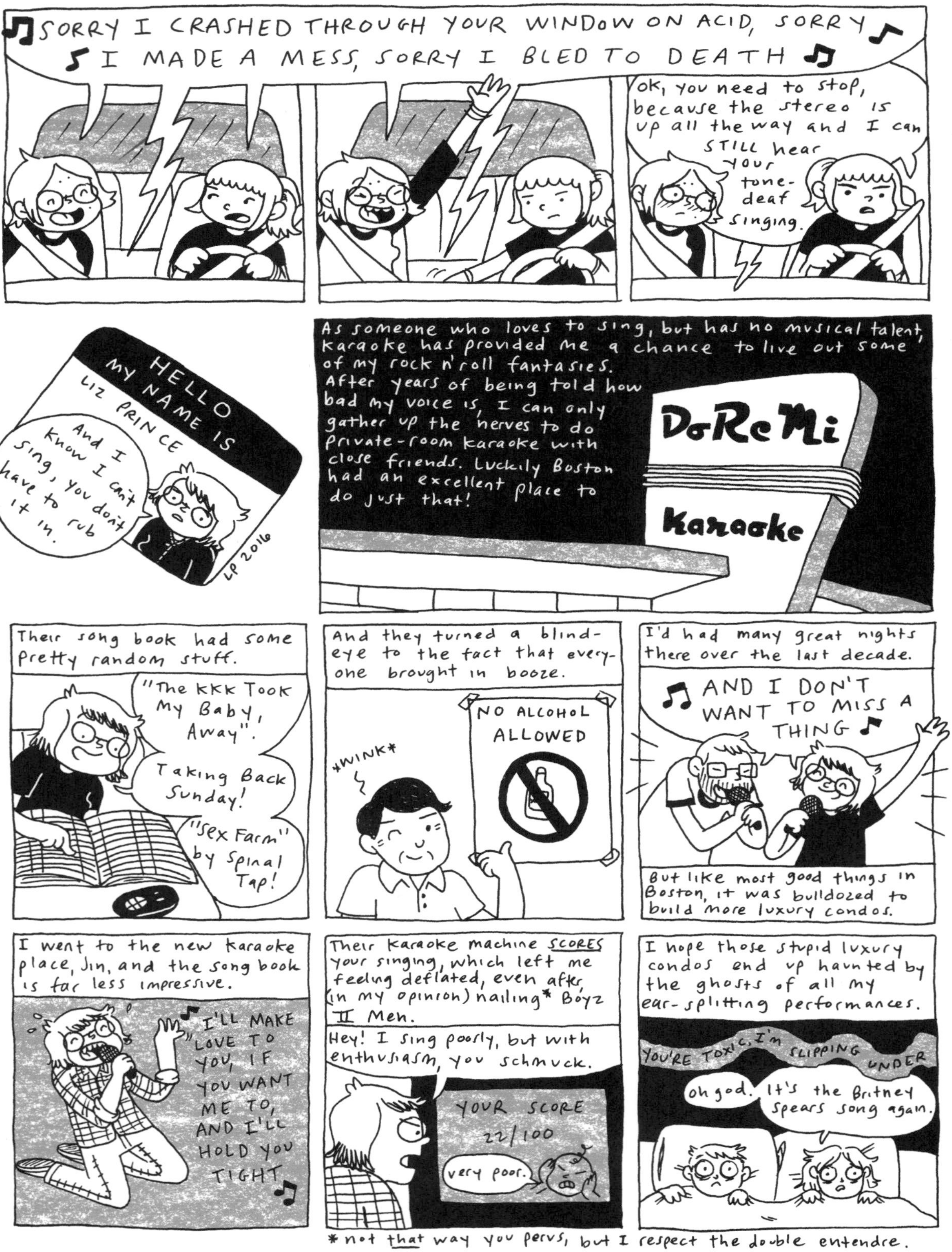
SORRY I CRASHED THROUGH YOUR WINDOW ON ACID, SORRY I MADE A MESS, SORRY I BLED TO DEATH
ok, you need to stop, because the stereo is up all the way and I can STILL hear your tone-deaf singing.
HELLO MY NAME IS LIZ PRINCE
And I know I can't sing, you don't have to rub it in.
LP 2016
As someone who loves to sing, but has no musical talent, karaoke has provided me a chance to live out some of my rock n' roll fantasies. After years of being told how bad my voice is, I can only gather up the nerves to do private-room karaoke with close friends. Luckily Boston had an excellent place to do just that!
DoReMi
Karaoke
Their song book had some pretty random stuff.
"The KKK Took My Baby Away".
Taking Back Sunday!
"Sex Farm" by Spinal Tap!
And they turned a blind-eye to the fact that everyone brought in booze.
WINK
NO ALCOHOL ALLOWED
I'd had many great nights there over the last decade.
AND I DON'T WANT TO MISS A THING
But like most good things in Boston, it was bulldozed to build more luxury condos.
I went to the new karaoke place, Jin, and the song book is far less impressive.
I'LL MAKE LOVE TO YOU, IF YOU WANT ME TO, AND I'LL HOLD YOU TIGHT
Their karaoke machine SCORES your singing, which left me feeling deflated, even after (in my opinion) nailing* Boyz II Men.
Hey! I sing poorly, but with enthusiasm, you schmuck.
YOUR SCORE 22/100
very poor.
I hope those stupid luxury condos end up haunted by the ghosts of all my ear-splitting performances.
YOU'RE TOXIC, I'M SLIPPING UNDER
Oh god. It's the Britney Spears song again.

* not that way you pervs, but I respect the double entendre.

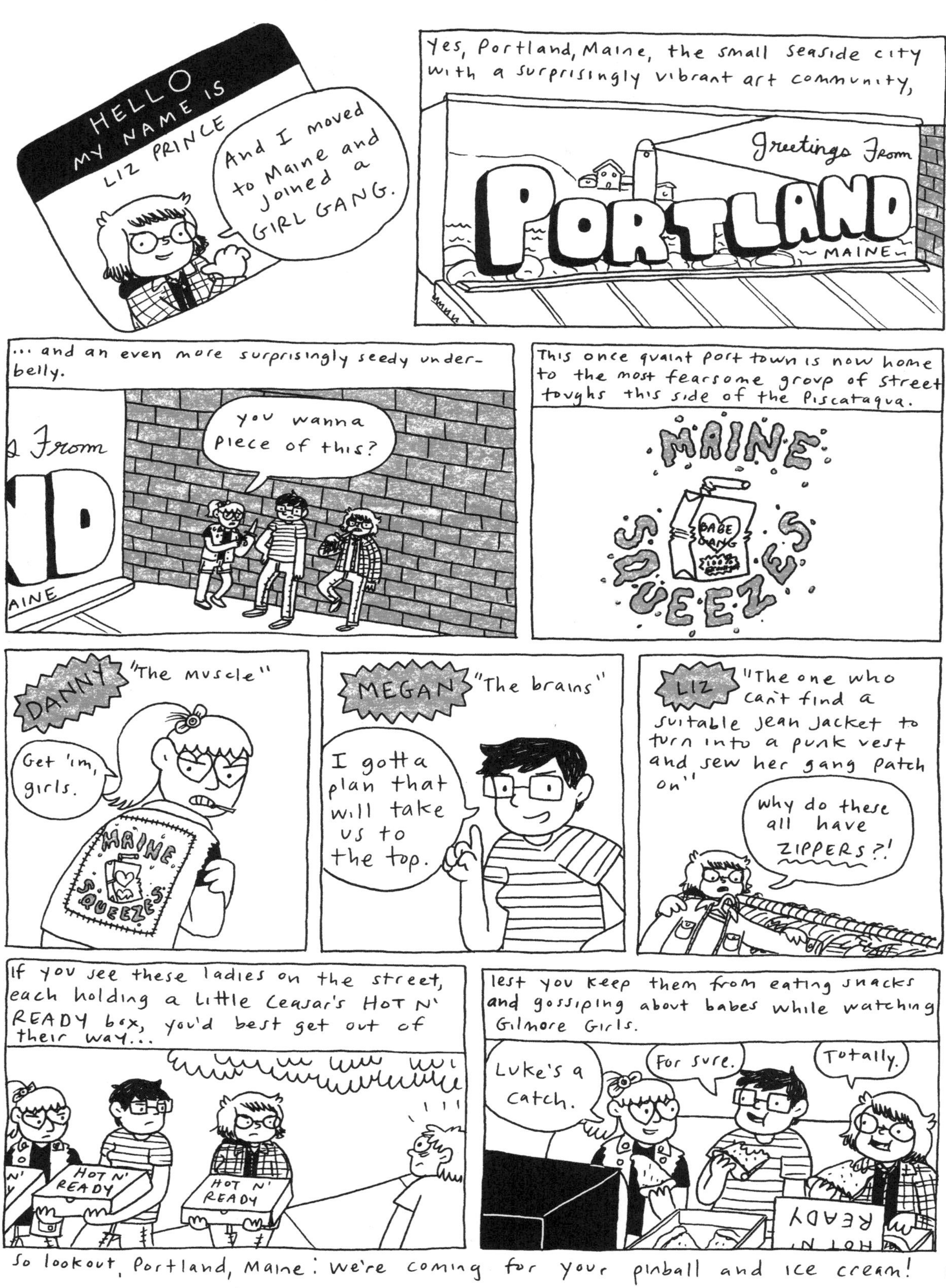
HELLO MY NAME IS
LIZ PRINCE
And I moved to Maine and joined a GIRL GANG.
Yes, Portland, Maine, the small seaside city with a surprisingly vibrant art community,
Greetings From
PORTLAND
MAINE
... and an even more surprisingly seedy underbelly.
You wanna piece of this?
This once quaint port town is now home to the most fearsome group of street toughs this side of the Piscataqua.
MAINE SQUEEZES
BABE GANG
DANNY "The muscle"
Get 'im, girls.
MAINE SQUEEZES
MEGAN "The brains"
I gotta plan that will take us to the top.
LIZ "The one who can't find a suitable jean jacket to turn into a punk vest and sew her gang patch on"
Why do these all have ZIPPERS?!
If you see these ladies on the street, each holding a Little Ceasar's HOT N' READY box, you'd best get out of their way...
HOT N' READY
HOT N' READY
lest you keep them from eating snacks and gossiping about babes while watching Gilmore Girls.
Luke's a catch.
For sure.
Totally.
HOT N' READY
So lookout, Portland, Maine: We're coming for your pinball and ice cream!

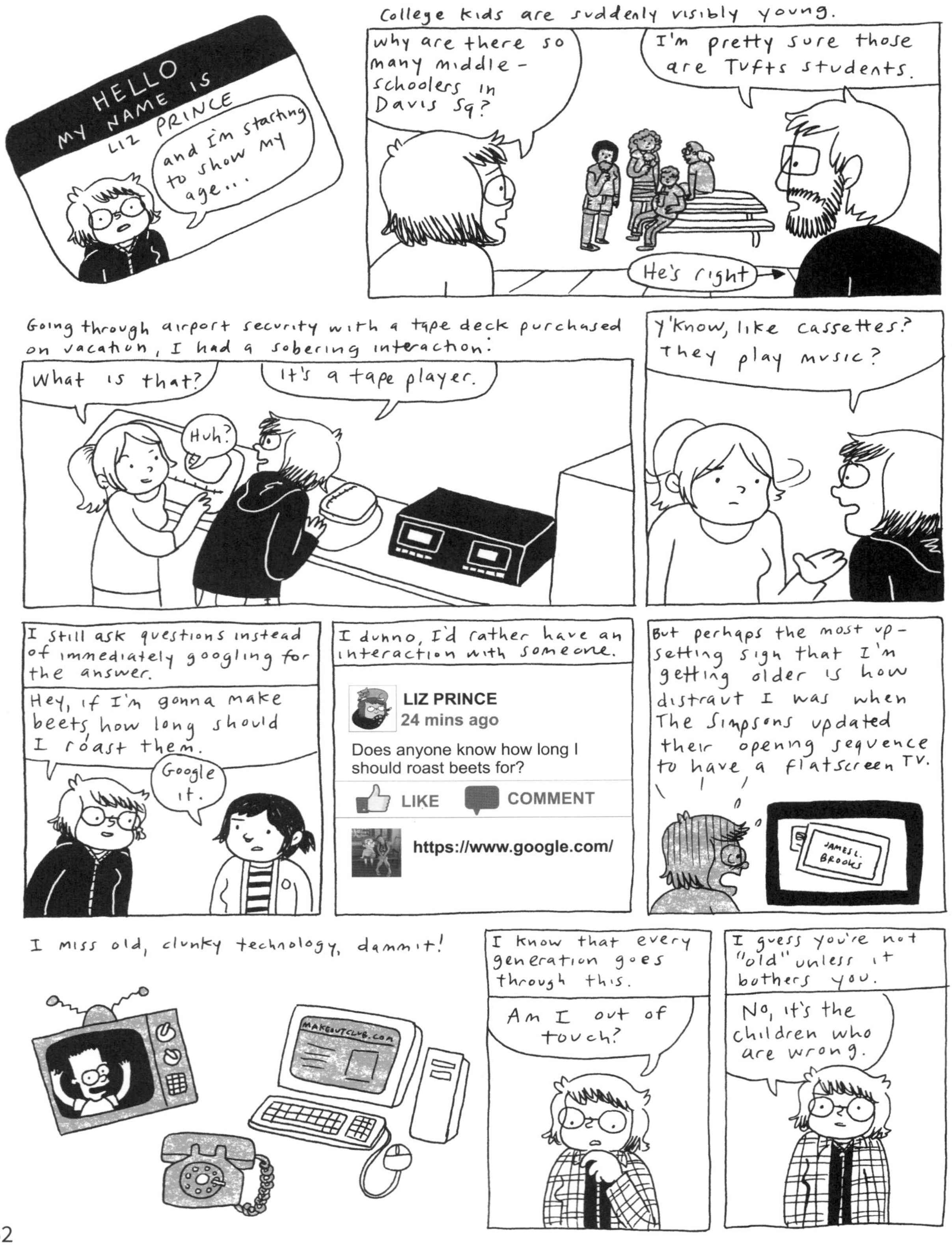
HELLO
MY NAME IS
LIZ PRINCE
and I'm starting to show my age...
College kids are suddenly visibly young.
why are there so many middle-schoolers in Davis Sq?
I'm pretty sure those are Tufts students.
He's right
Going through airport security with a tape deck purchased on vacation, I had a sobering interaction:
What is that?
It's a tape player.
Huh?
Y'know, like cassettes? They play music?
I still ask questions instead of immediately googling for the answer.
Hey, if I'm gonna make beets, how long should I roast them.
Google it.
I dunno, I'd rather have an interaction with someone.
LIZ PRINCE
24 mins ago
Does anyone know how long I should roast beets for?
LIKE
COMMENT
https://www.google.com/
But perhaps the most upsetting sign that I'm getting older is how distraut I was when The Simpsons updated their opening sequence to have a flatscreen TV.
JAMES L. BROOKS
I miss old, clunky technology, dammit!
MAKEOUTCLUB.COM
I know that every generation goes through this.
Am I out of touch?
I guess you're not "old" unless it bothers you.
No, it's the children who are wrong.

NOTES

pg.14-18 My Chaos in Tejas Diary

This 4 page comic diary of my trip to Chaos in Tejas in 2010 received a lot of flack online because of how "wimpy" it was (common complaints were that I only saw the worst bands/ had too much extra curriculars: not even of the punx), but that was actually the tongue-in-cheek point of the comic! I called it diary, and dotted the I with a heart to drive that point home. Oh well, haters be damned, because I'm still here!

Pg.26-30 Ergs! Reunion

This comic about the Ergs! reunion in 2010 was drawn in collaboration with my good friend Jim Kettner! We went to the show together (actually the first time we'd hung out in many years!), and then drew worked on the resulting 4 pages together over the course of 3 days that I spent in Philly afterwards. We each wrote our own 1-page lead-ins to the comic, and then we drew the 2 pages about the actual show in tandem. Unfortunately I only had half the pages, and couldn't obtain a high(er) res scan of the 4th page, so I apologize if the image quality is noticeably different.

Pg.38 - My Stupid Vacation

Another collaboration strip, this time with Razorcake alumni Mitch Clem and Amanda Kirk! I visited Mitch and Amanda in San Antonio, and forced them to draw this comic with me: they penciled themselves in, and then I inked the entire thing, which ended up looking a little less slick than I'd hoped, but it was a fun experiment none-the-less. The comic is named after Mitch's now defunct autobio series My Stupid Life, which was named after a Mr. T Experience song, which might have been named after something else, but now we're going too far down the rabbit hole.

Pg.53 - Girls Rule

I just want to stress that I could have listed about 100 women that have personally ruled in my life, but I ran out of space and time, so if you know me, and you don't see your name on there, just know that it's nothing personal!

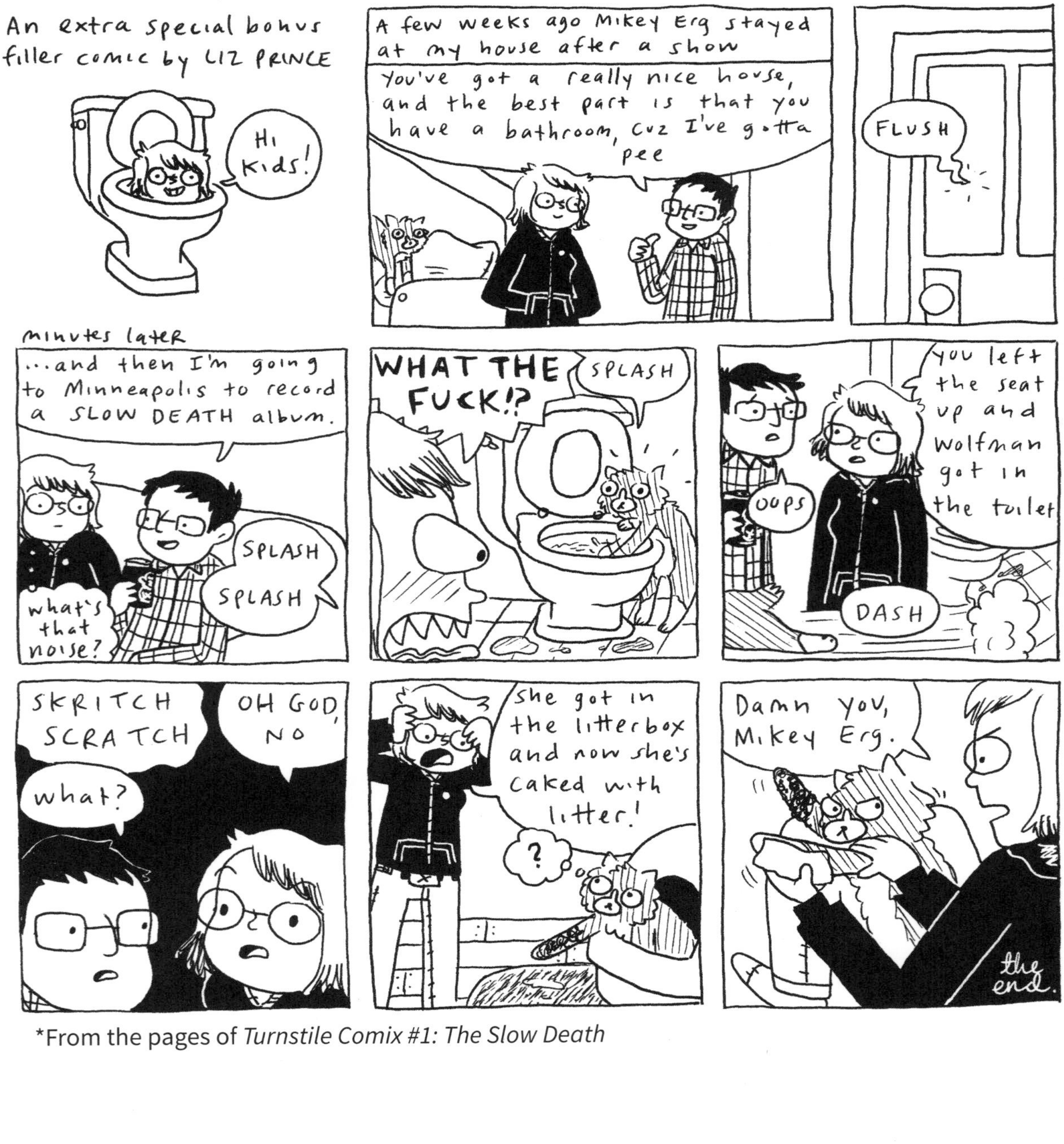
An extra special bonus filler comic by LIZ PRINCE
Hi kids!
A few weeks ago Mikey Erg stayed at my house after a show
You've got a really nice house, and the best part is that you have a bathroom, cuz I've gotta pee
FLUSH
minutes later
...and then I'm going to Minneapolis to record a SLOW DEATH album.
SPLASH
SPLASH
what's that noise?
WHAT THE FUCK!?
SPLASH
You left the seat up and Wolfman got in the toilet
OOPS
DASH
SKRITCH SCRATCH
OH GOD, NO
what?
She got in the litterbox and now she's caked with litter!
?
Damn you, Mikey Erg.
the end.

*From the pages of *Turnstile Comix #1: The Slow Death*

ABOUT THE AUTHOR

Oh jeez, you haven't heard enough about Liz already?

I mean, all of these stupid comics were about her…

Ok, fine, I guess you just want more, and I don't blame you.

Liz Prince grew up in Santa Fe, New Mexico, immersing herself in the great DIY scene surrounding Warehouse 21, a teen art center unlike any other.

In addition to her comics in this book, she has drawn comics for *Adventure Time*, *Regular Show*, *Garfield*, and numerous zines and anthologies, including the celebrated punk comics anthology *As You Were*, edited by Mitch Clem and published by Silver Sprocket.

Liz's previous books include the Ignatz-award winning *Will You Still Love Me If I Wet the Bed?*, *Alone Forever*, and the critically-acclaimed *Tomboy: A Graphic Memoir*. Her newest project is a comic series called *Coady and The Creepies*, which is being drawn by the incomparable Nation Of Amanda (Kirk).

Liz lives in Portland, Maine, with her cats Wolfman & Dracula, and her husband Kyle. She belongs to a girl gang called the Maine Squeezes, and plays in an all-women pinball league. Yes, she really is that cool.

Visit www.lizprincepower.com to get up-to-the-minute updates on her life and comics.

THANK YOUS

Thanks to Dave Garwacke of www.ifyoumakeit.com for getting me started on this long-standing project of drawing comics (loosely) around the theme of music by inviting me to contribute to his website back in 2009. Even though there hasn't been a new post in several years, there is still a hefty backlog of live videos, full albums to download, comics (not just by me!), and the site's signature Pink Couch Sessions, so give it a visit whydontcha.

Thanks to Todd Taylor at Razorcake for giving these comics a home in print; the internet is cool and all, but I'd always rather see my work on paper. Can you believe that Razorcake has been going strong for 16 years! If you visit www.razorcake.org you can read archived issues of the magazine, listen to podcasts by contributors, subscribe to the print issues (yes, you should), and see new punk comics every wednesday by a variety of artists.

Thanks to Mitch Clem for being my in at Razorcake.

To everyone who was portrayed in these comics, thanks for being my friend and letting me write about our experiences and/or your band. Special thanks to Jim Kettner, Mitch Clem, Amanda Kirk and Tony Pence, for collaborating and/or appearing in some of these comics (or in Tony's case, putting up with me drawing us smooching). I am eternally grateful to Justin Mulkern for reigniting my interest in pop punk, which is kind of how I ended up with this book in the first place!

And finally, to Avi at Silver Sprocket: sorry it took me a full fucking year to get this together. Thanks for your patience, and for continuing to put out cutting edge punk art. I still have lots of copies of your old Springman Records comps that I failed to adequately distribute back in the early-aughts, so yes, I'm a terrible person, but I mean well!

Maine Squeezes por vida!

ESSENTIAL COMIX FROM SILVER SPROCKET

Each volume of **As You Were** collects self-contained short stories by our favorite punk rocker comic artists from all over the world. The latest is Vol. 5, This Job Sucks (#SILVER065). Also available: Vol. 1, House Shows (#SILVER045); Vol. 3, Big, Big Changes (#SILVER052); Vol. 4, Living Situations (#SILVER060). 5.5"x8.5", b&w

ANONYMOUS
Our Best Shot
The secret story of a Supervised Injection Facility operating illegally against the USA's disastrous "War On Drugs." *#SILVER067, 30 pages, 5.5"x8.5" b&w*

JENN WOODALL
Magical Beatdown
Hyper-violent Sailor Moon inspired action anime street-harassment revenge fantasy comic printed in blue and fluorescent pink risograph. #SILVER068 (44 pages, 5"x 7")

BEN PASSMORE
Your Black Friend
An open letter from your black friend about race, racism, friendship, and alienation. *#SILVER066, 12 pages, 5.5"x8.5" full-color*

MICHAEL SWEATER
Please Destroy My Enemies
Witty and irreverent funny comics by a skater/tagger/punk raised on Calvin and Hobbes, The Far Side and Foxtrot. Funny, cute and disturbing comics, all too relatable and gut wrenchingly hilarious. #SILVER064, 60 pages, 6"x6" b&w

BEN PASSMORE
Goodbye
It's hard to say goodbye to love, to friends, to ourselves. Our identity is a myth we make. Goodbye includes a myth about polyamory, a parable about real punks, and an argument for aging gracefully (or killing yourself). *#SILVER062, 88 pages, 4" x 5.5" b&w*

IO 'CLAST & RACHEL DUKES
No Gods. No Dungeon Masters
An analysis of multi-classing between nerd and anarchist subcultures. *#SILVER071, 12 pages, 5.5"x8.5" full-color*

JAMES THE STANTON
Squatters of Trash Island The new off-shore anthropology *#SILVER072, 20 pages, 5.5"x8.5" full-color*

Turnstile Comix by **MITCH CLEM** & **NATION OF AMANDA** contain the shouldn't-be-true tour stories from our favorite bands as 40 page comics with a 7" EP of new songs on colored vinyl. **The World/Inferno Friendship Society** (#SILVER041) inspires with dazzling tales of anarchic chaos and fighting Snapcase.
Lemuria (#SILVER056) tours Russia to face mobsters, crooked cops, Nazis, and cute diseased dogs. 7"x7" b&w

COMING SOON

New books, comics and zines by favorites
BEAU PATRICK COULON, BENJI NATE, BEN PASSMORE, FERIN FICK, ISABELLA ROTMAN, JAMES THE STANTON, JENN WOODALL, LIZ PRINCE, LIZ SUBURBIA, MICHAEL SWEATER, MITCH CLEM, NATION OF AMANDA, NOEL'LE LONGHAUL, RACHEL DUKES, TOM NEELY, and **WILL LAREN**

Shop direct online:
http://store.silversprocket.net/zines

WE MAKE COMICS AND GEAR WITH OUR FAVORITE ARTIST BUDS LIKE ANDY WARNER, BEN PASSMORE, FERIN FICK, IO 'CLAST, JENN WOODALL, JOSHUM, LAUREN MONGER, LINDSAY WATSON, LIZ PRINCE, LIZ SUBURBIA, MEG HAS ISSUES, MICHAEL SWEATER, MITCH CLEM, NATION OF AMANDA, RACHEL DUKES, SARAH DUYER, AND WILL LAREN

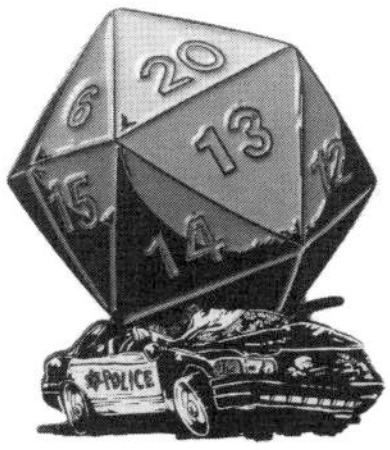
20
6
13
15
14
12
POLICE

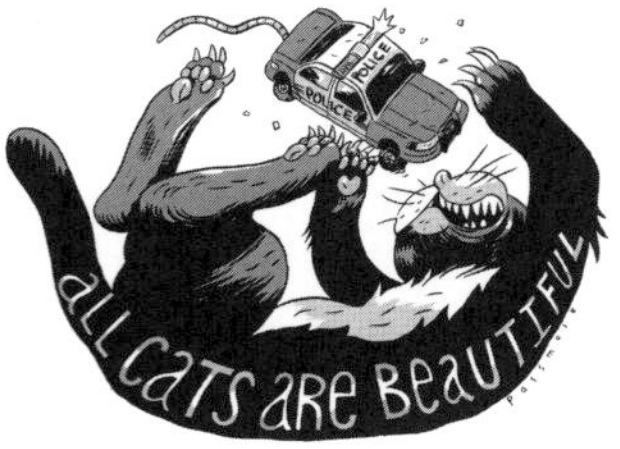
POLICE
all cats are beautiful

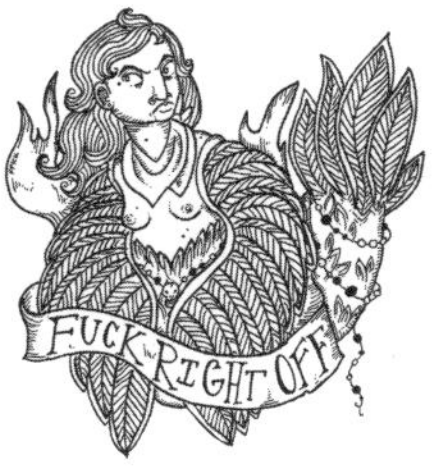
FUCK RIGHT OFF

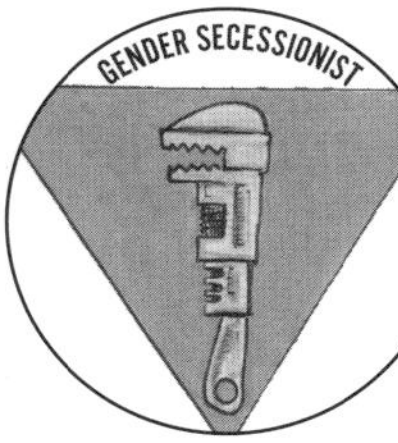
GENDER SECESSIONIST

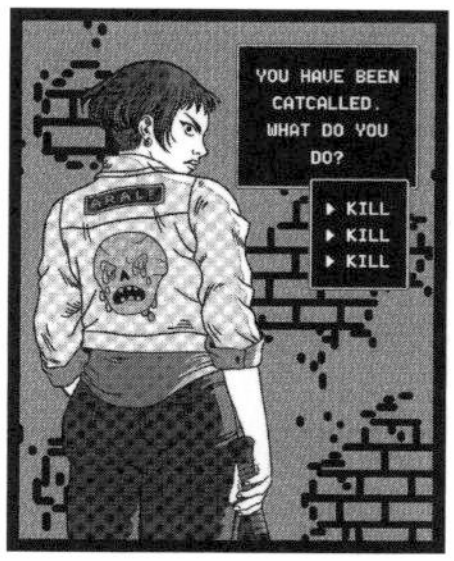
YOU HAVE BEEN CATCALLED. WHAT DO YOU DO?
▶ KILL
▶ KILL
▶ KILL

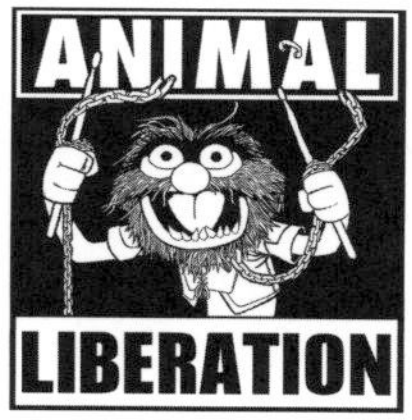
ANIMAL
LIBERATION

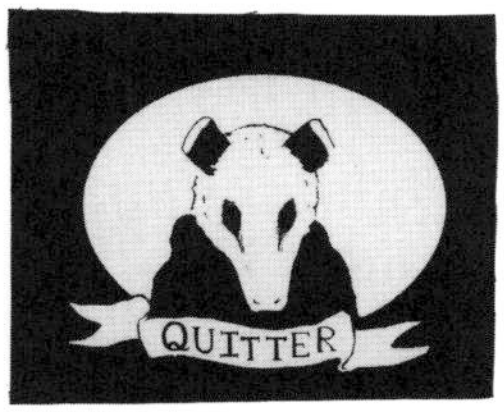
QUITTER

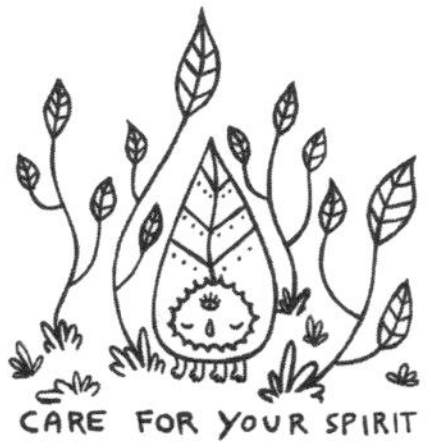
CARE FOR YOUR SPIRIT

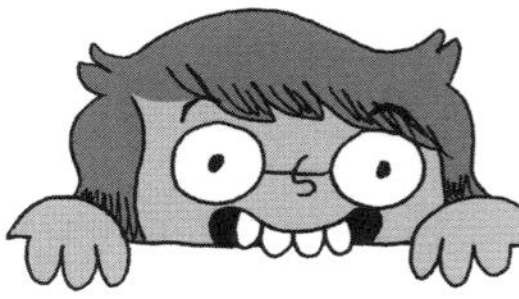

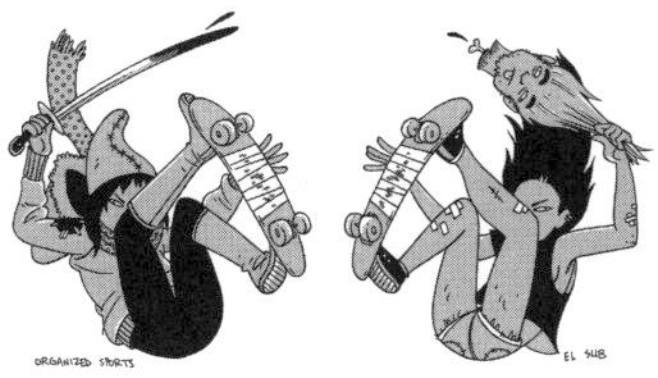
ORGANIZED SPORTS
EL SUB

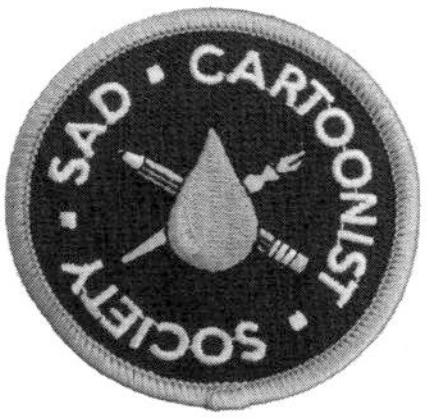
SAD · CARTOONIST · SOCIETY ·

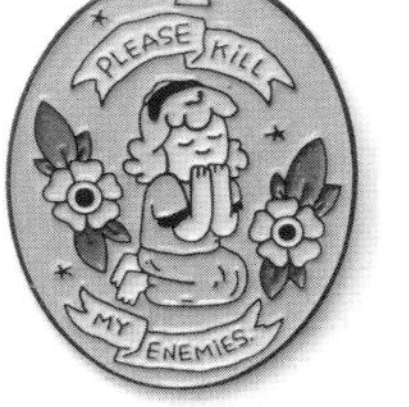
PLEASE KILL
MY ENEMIES.

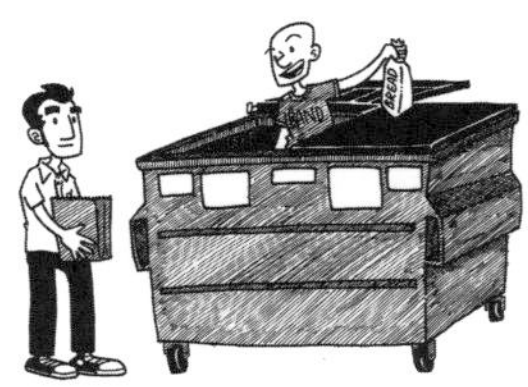

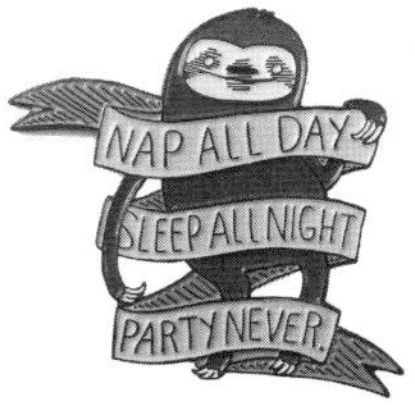
NAP ALL DAY
SLEEP ALL NIGHT
PARTY NEVER.

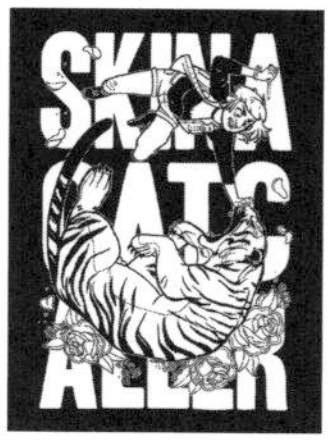

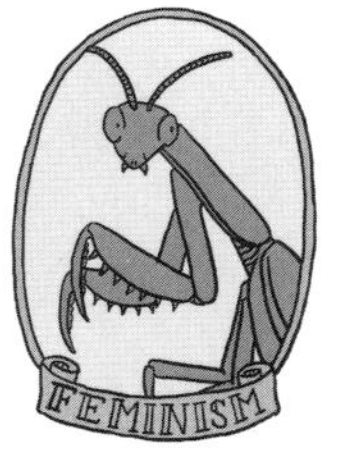
FEMINISM

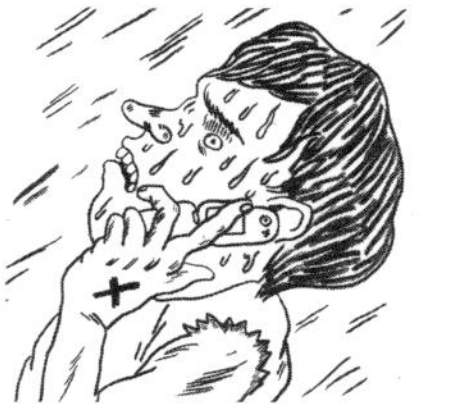

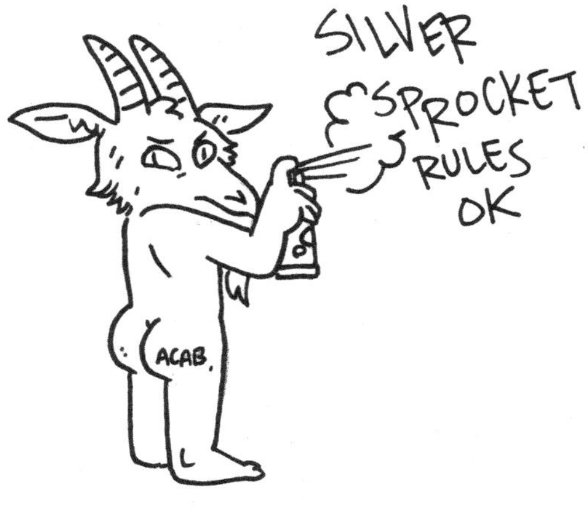
SILVER SPROCKET RULES OK
ACAB.

Silver Sprocket is a bicycle club, art crew, publisher, record label, and group of buds being self sustained disasters.

Being a tiny bedroom & basement operation, word-of-mouth is the main way people find out about these artists and projects.

You sharing this with friends and posting about it online goes a long way and is way appreciated.

Visit our website for news, comics, events, shenanigans, a list of retailers who carry our gear, and our direct online shop:

www.silversprocket.net

Instagram @silversprocket, Twitter @ssbcpunk, facebook.com/silversprocket, bandcamp.silversprocket.net, tumblr.SilverSprocket.net

Thanks for your support!